Ferns

D0762617

CALGARY PUBLIC LIBRARY

DEC / / 2003

Ferns

Martin Rickard

THE ROYAL HORTICULTURAL SOCIETY

Text © Martin Rickard 2003
All rights reserved

The right of Martin Rickard to be identified as the author of
this work has been asserted by him in accordance with the
Copyright, Designs and Patents Act 1988.

First published in Great Britain in 2003 by
Cassell Illustrated
Octopus Publishing Group
2–4 Heron Quays, London E14 4JP

A CIP record for this book is available
from the British Library

ISBN 1 84403 063 6

Commissioning Editor: Camilla Stoddart
Editor: Robin Douglas-Withers
Designer: Justin Hunt
Illustrator: Patrick Mulrey

Jacket Image © Garden Picture Library/Clive Boursnell
All photographs are reproduced courtesy of the author, except
p.63 (left) by Gordon Rae.

Printed in China

CONTENTS

Previous page:
Athyrium niponicum
'Pictum', ramose form,
shown here with
Cyrtomium fortunei
to left.

INTRODUCTION

When I first became interested in ferns and fern growing in the late 1960s the fern world could boast two giants: Jimmy Dyce (later MBE), who looked after the British Pteridological Society, and Reginald Kaye, who ran the only real fern nursery. Sadly, neither is with us today, but both lived into their nineties. In 1968 Reginald Kaye wrote the seminal *Hardy Ferns*, and a few years later, in 1978, published the excellent *Ferns* (Wisley Handbook number 32). The latter is, of course, long out of print and, inevitably, now largely out of date. This new book is over twice the size of its predecessor so I hope it will not only fill the void but also significantly add to the basic information required to grow ferns, in variety and to perfection. Although slim, this book contains information on most of the ferns available in commerce today.

HISTORY OF FERN GROWING

Ferns have long been noted by botanists and gardeners. *Polypodium australe* 'Cambricum' was found in Wales in 1668 and is still in cultivation today known as 'Richard Kayse', but for a hundred years or so, there were few other notable discoveries, and ferns were grown rarely, if at all.

It was in the 18th century that ferns began to be more widely appreciated. They were used to adorn grottoes and woodland situations in larger estates, although plantings in small gardens were still rare. Early in the reign of Queen Victoria, however, a growing interest in their natural history led to frequent forays in search of the different kinds. Many

Polypodium australe 'Richard Kayse', the original 'Cambricum'.

6

specimens were dug up and brought home as souvenirs of country holidays and, sad to say, some species suffered due to over-enthusiastic collecting, especially near railway stations. The wardian case, invented by Nathaniel Ward in 1840, in part stimulated this interest in ferns. Really little more than a fish tank with a glass roof (but not filled with water), this provided a good environment for the ferns to grow in – the virtually sealed unit kept the humidity up and the toxic town atmosphere out, both to the advantage of the ferns.

Collectors were much aided by books written by George Francis (*An Analysis of British Fern and their Allies*, 1837) and Edward Newman (*A History of British Ferns*, 1840 and 1844). Although these mainly detailed the species, with a few cultivars, they also gave tempting descriptions of where the ferns grew (125 years later I was able to follow up Newman's information with some success!).

In the mid–19th century the Victorian fern craze really took off. Newman's revised edition of his book (1854) included more records of wild cultivar finds, and numerous other books were written, the best by Thomas Moore and, later, Edward Lowe. Sadly, Newman and Moore fell out, as Newman accused Moore of plagiarism (rightly in my view). In 1855, while based at the Chelsea Physic Garden in London, Moore, who had recovered from the earlier scandal, published *The Ferns of Great Britain and Ireland*. Probably the finest ever work on ferns, this is a beautiful nature-printed folio edition, probably now worth in excess of £3000.

The cover of A History of British Ferns (1854) by Edward Newman.

As the century progressed, more books were published and more ferns collected, and cultivars were increasingly among them. Around 1860 most of these cultivars were of a minor type that would not be kept by growers today; there were, however, some exceptionally good ones, a few of which are still in cultivation. By the end of the century, interest in fern growing was decreasing. Curiously, this coincided with an increase in the raising and discovery of more and more really good cultivars. Those who remained devoted to the subject formed the British Pteridological Society (1891) and the American Fern Society (1893). These devotees were very energetic and, though few in number, raised many new forms and kept large collections. Whilst they remained largely unaffected by the First World War, many reached old age and died during the Second World War. As a consequence the fern cult suffered a serious setback, and had it not been for the efforts of Jimmy Dyce around 1948, the British Pteridological Society would have closed. Jimmy succeeded in rebuilding the society into the much stronger organization that flourishes today. His work resulted in ferns recovering their public popularity, as can be seen by their frequent use in television garden makeovers and their increasing presence at RHS shows.

It is interesting to note that one of the first recorded wild fern cultivars in Britain was discovered in the reign of King Charles II, and that this cultivar is now among many others in the garden of the Patron of the British Pteridological Society – Prince Charles.

THE BEAUTY OF FERNS

Ferns may seem a little homogenous to the uninitiated, but there are a number of very good reasons why they are becoming quite widely grown in Europe and North America. These include colour, form and texture.

Dryopteris neorosthornii.

Although most ferns are green, there are at least 40 shades of green – dark greens, pale greens, matt greens, glossy greens, blue-greens, yellow greens, and so on – and there are also other colours. In *Athyrium* colours include greys and purples; red, cinnamon and yellow occur in *Osmunda*; *Cyathea* has silver and black, while in *Dryopteris* (below) there is black, red and brown, and many eastern Asian species, have red fronds when young.

Ferns have a wonderful range of form: from the dwarf rock species, such as *Asplenium trichomanes*, to the spectacular tree ferns, such as *Dicksonia antarctica*, no other group of plants can match their simple elegance. They create a restful atmosphere in the garden; one year at the Chelsea Flower Show I noticed a man gazing at the ferns on display for quite a while. Eventually I asked if I could help, but apparently he was just resting his eyes!

Frond texture varies widely. In any mixed fern planting I always recommend the inclusion of different frond types; for example, *Asplenium scolopendrium* with its strap-shaped fronds is excellent intermingled with filigree ferns such as *Dryopteris filix-mas*: the contrast between the two kinds is stunning, and the larger the planting the better the effect.

Ferns have a long season. In virtually all, the fronds remain attractive for at least six months and in some cases all year. Compare this to herbaceous plants, few of which flower for longer than a month or two.

Two evergreen ferns: Polypodium glycyrrhiza 'Longicaudatum' with Asplenium scolopendrium 'Bolton's Nobile' behind.

Most ferns are easy to grow. The majority of the taxa described here make good garden plants as long as they are given shade and their moisture and temperature requirements are taken into consideration. Over 220 taxa have been included, 60 of them having obtained the Award of Garden Merit (AGM), which means they are considered by the Royal Horticultural Society's specialists to be plants of outstanding quality, in both appearance and all round garden performance.

Finally, for the scientifically orientated, ferns make a fascinating study. They are the most primitive group of vascular plants – many are living fossils – and in addition have a complicated lifecycle that only came to be understood just over a century ago.

Ferns have few economic uses although some parts are edible, notably the fiddleheads (young croziers) of *Matteuccia pensylvanica*, which are eaten in North America. (They are reputed to taste like asparagus, but, having tried them, give me asparagus any time!) Their principal value must be as garden plants where they are now more popular than at any time since the middle of the Victorian era.

Carcinogenic?

I believe that carcinogens have only been proven in bracken, which I would not recommend as a garden plant. The longevity of so many fern growers would suggest we have little need to worry perhaps the relaxation generated by their cultivation counters any toxins?

FERN NAMES

At species level, fern names are decided by international botanists, rarely by gardeners, although we may have our own opinions (see *Polypodium australe* for mine!) Conversely, cultivar names are usually decided by horticulturalists, often the raiser or finder. In this situation there are some rules that have to be obeyed. Principally, since 1 January, 1959, fern names have to be in a living language, that is, not Latin or Ancient Greek. This scheme arose in part as a result of the difficulty of separating Latin species names from Latin cultivar names, but more importantly to stop the proliferation of excessively long descriptive names, such as *Polystichum setiferum* 'Plumoso-divisilobum Deltoideum', which is legal because it was first used long before 1959 but could not be applied today. Similar problems occurred in other groups, such as conifers. Those simply dabbling in ferns will no doubt be pleased to see the end of such names, but traditionalists like me regret it: the descriptive name *Polystichum setiferum* 'Plumoso-divisilobum Deltoideum' tells me exactly what to expect of the plant, whereas a fancy name like, perhaps, *Polystichum setiferum* 'John Smith' says nothing about it, except that someone called John Smith is connected with it. A concession to the 'old school' has been to introduce a 'Group' concept, which entails placing a cultivar in a group where appropriate. In the above example, our fern might be *Polystichum setiferum* (Plumoso-divisilobum Group) 'John Smith'. The section in brackets is not part of the name, and can be omitted legally, but it is a useful guide.

With ferns these issues are mainly confined to rare clones, which are outside the scope of this book. Of more relevance here is the use of group names to list the spore progeny of cultivars. Owing to genetic recombination, some cultivars do not come true from spores. *Athyrium filix-femina* 'Victoriae' is a good example: its progeny is close but not the same as the parent. So the group system comes into play – we can refer to all sporelings of 'Victoriae' as Cruciatum Group. However, if one of the sporelings proves good enough to justify vegetative reproduction, including by tissue culture, a clone can be named: for example, *A. filix-femina* (Cruciatum group) 'Lady Victoria' or, simply, *A. filix-femina* 'Lady Victoria'.

Many of the old Latin names are still current on cultivars named before 1959; they are also often used in group names. The most commonly encountered are explained in the glossary. For a full listing see *Fern Names and their Meanings* (James Dyce, 1988).

Recently the use of hyphens in plant names has been discouraged, but this is not universally popular and has not been accepted here. Plumoso-divisilobum or Bifido-grandiceps is bad enough but surely Plumosodivisilobum or Bifidograndiceps is worse?

WHAT IS A FERN?

Ferns are vascular cryptogams, the most primitive group of vascular plants and the most advanced group of cryptogams; vascular plants include conifers and flowering plants, while cryptogams include mosses, liverworts and algae. At the time of the dinosaurs, ferns and their allies were the dominant plant group on earth. There are approximately 10,000 species of fern and fern allies worldwide. (Fern allies include clubmosses, horsetails and quillworts.) Most species diversity occurs in tropical rainforests.

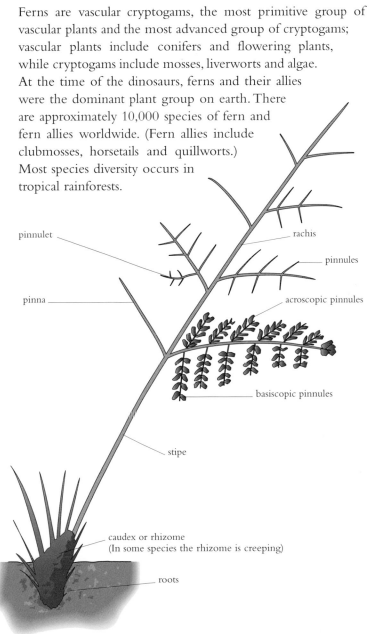

pinnulet

rachis

pinnules

pinna

acroscopic pinnules

basiscopic pinnules

stipe

caudex or rhizome
(In some species the rhizome is creeping)

roots

Ferns reproduce sexually by spores, which are usually produced on the underside of the frond and may be black, brown or green. Green spores are shortlived and need to be sown within a few days of shedding. Spores of other colours are often viable even one year after collection, although the germination rate declines with time. In the absence of flowers, fern identification at generic level is based on the structure of the sorus. At species and cultivar level other basic features are critical, such as frond shape and margin and frond dissection. Terms for these features are shown below; additional technical terms are explained in the glossary.

Explanation of terms for frond shape

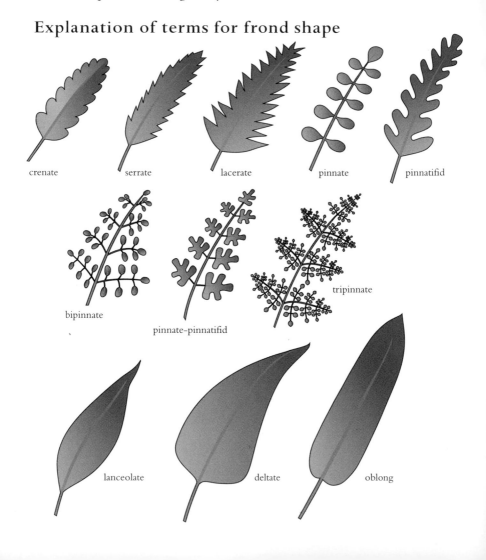

crenate   serrate   lacerate   pinnate   pinnatifid

bipinnate   pinnate-pinnatifid   tripinnate

lanceolate   deltate   oblong

Typical fern life cycle

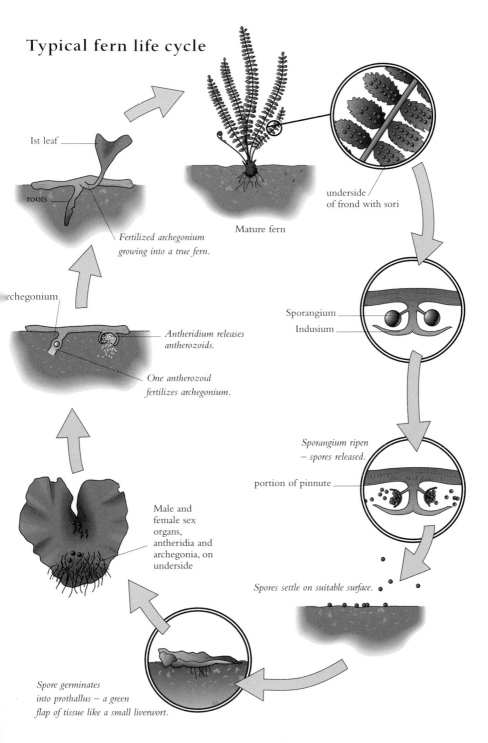

1st leaf

roots

Fertilized archegonium growing into a true fern.

Mature fern

underside of frond with sori

archegonium

Antheridium releases antherozoids.

One antherozoid fertilizes archegonium.

Sporangium

Indusium

Sporangium ripen – spores released.

portion of pinnute

Male and female sex organs, antheridia and archegonia, on underside

Spores settle on suitable surface.

Spore germinates into prothallus – a green flap of tissue like a small liverwort.

CULTIVATION OF FERNS

Ferns are unexpectedly easy to grow, but the following factors influence their luxuriance.

SITE

Ferns like plenty of light but not too much direct sun, which can scorch them: shade or dappled shade is ideal. Some will grow in full sun, notably species of *Cheilanthes*, and many that prefer shade will survive in full sun for much of the day but are rarely as impressive in such a situation. I recommend avoiding sites that are in full sun in midsummer from noon until 3pm. Sun at other times of the day is fine. Ferns do not like wind, but shady or dappled sites are not usually too windy.

If you are trying a species that is only borderline hardy in your district, plant it beside a rock, with the roots, and possibly the crown, just under the rock. Alternatively, in the autumn, place a handful of straw over the crown and weigh it down with a stone; remove the stone in the spring. Tree ferns are a special case (p.33–35).

WATER

Most ferns like well-drained soil, but some like it wet; particular requirements are given in the individual descriptions (p.39–81). In the wild most species choose to grow on shady banks, where the soil neither dries out nor gets waterlogged. Try not to water too often: frequent applications of small amounts of water encourage surface rooting; infrequent thorough soakings are better. However, it is not always that easy – when a plant looks

Matteuccia struthiopteris, somewhat yellowed by being in full sun, at RHS Garden Rosemoor in Devon.

– when a plant looks thirsty I can never resist watering it! Watering can be reduced by mulching in the spring.

Bog ferns can be a problem in well-drained gardens. To overcome this, excavate an area to a depth of 15cm (6in), lay old compost bags or plastic sheeting all over the bottom, then refill with the old soil improved with leaf mould. Even in droughts this should keep moist. It enabled me to grow osmundas to a good size in any garden.

SOIL

Soil is not critical. Very free-draining soils can be difficult as frequent watering may be necessary, but ferns love moist sand. Clay is fine; it is hard to work but rarely dries out completely. Good loam is perfect, although a slight disadvantage over clay is that it dries out more quickly. Stony soils are great, as ferns love to have the cool root run that can be found under stones. Ferns also love organic matter in the soil, so add well-rotted garden compost, leaf mould or other organic material to new fern beds.

Acidity is rarely a problem. A few ferns do not like lime – *Blechnum, Oreopteris, Cryptogramma crispa*, for example – and all seem to be able to grow in its absence, although *Asplenium scolopendrium* does not thrive without it.

FERTILIZER

I rarely fertilize my garden ferns. They do fine. No doubt they could be bigger, but a well-fertilized luxuriant specimen will need more water when a drought comes along. In pots, ferns do need feeding. I use slow-release granules in the compost in all nursery stock and then revert to watering-on any general-purpose product once the granules have run out of steam; or I sometimes sprinkle slow-release granules over the compost surface, relying on the watering to distribute the feed.

FERNS IN POTS

Most ferns can be grown in pots, but it is a more labour-intensive process than growing them in an open bed. Like those in beds, they prefer some shelter from the wind and a shady site. Feeding is necessary (see above), but the biggest problem is getting the watering right.

Ferns classified as dry–wet in the descriptions (p.39–81) need a free-draining compost and should never be allowed to get waterlogged. Equally, they should never dry out: hence they require frequent watering in the growing season, but should never be left standing in a tray of water for more than a few minutes. In less than ideal conditions I prefer to let these ferns get too dry rather than too wet. With nursing, dry ferns often recover, but many of those that have got too wet will rot and die. To help drainage, I add grit to the compost and place crocks at the bottom of the pot.

Cryptogramma crispa is a fern for lime-free soil.

Ferns classified as wet–dry are easier to grow in pots because they are easier to water – they are rarely overwatered. With real water lovers, such as osmundas, stand them in trays of water which are topped up as soon as the level drops.

General-purpose compost is fine for most ferns, especially if you can incorporate some well-rotted garden compost or leaf mould since they like some organic matter in their soil. For lime-hating ferns use ericaceous compost.

MAINTENANCE

Once established, ferns need little attention apart from watering in drought. In early spring it is a good idea, but not essential, to remove dead fronds before the new growth starts. This effectively reduces the chances for diseases to carry over from one season to the next, and it looks tidier. If they are left until too late, removing them without damaging the new growth can be a tedious business.

Many garden ferns can survive with low maintenance for a century or more if given ideal conditions at the start. I have visited Victorian fern gardens where huge plants of *Polystichum* and *Osmunda* still thrive. Sometimes, usually in drier sites, the caudex of a long-standing fern can grow out of the soil like a small trunk. In the short term this is very attractive, but in time the plant will die from dehydration. I recommend scaping soil up against the caudex, or lifting the whole plant and planting it slightly deeper. This can be partly achieved by mulching with well-rotted garden compost, leaf mould or other organic matter, which has the added benefit of improving the soil.

PROPAGATION

From spores

There are many ways to propagate ferns, but the only way to raise large numbers at once is by spores. This technique has one big disadvantage: because it is a sexual technique, it allows for genetic recombination, which in turn means that cultivars often do not come true; however, on the plus side, there is always the potential for a really exciting new break. At first glance the process might seem somewhat time consuming, but it is quite straight forward as long as the fern's lifecycle is understood.

First, collect your spores. Examine the plant for sporing fronds – in most species the spores are borne on the under surface. In most common genera, such as *Dryopteris*, *Athyrium*, *Asplenium* and *Polystichum*, spores ripen in summer. Select a frond with sori and, using a hand lens, inspect it to see if the dozens of sporangia that make up each sorus are round or chaffy (i.e. shaggy). If round and dark, they will soon burst open, if green, they are probably not ripe, although there are some exceptions, such as *Osmunda* (see p.67); chaffy sori have already shed. Collect a few pinnules on which you believe the sporangia are ripe and put them in a paper envelope; seal them in and keep dry for two days or so. If you do not have a hand lens or are unsure whether the sporangia are ripe, it is a good idea to collect pinnae at intervals along a frond and, indeed, pinnae from different fronds; this way you greatly increase the chances of getting some ripe spores.

Next, prepare the growing medium. Fill 7cm (3in) pots to the brim with compost and place on a stout tray. The type of compost seems not to matter but I tend to prefer ericaceous. Firm and smooth the compost then completely soak the surface with boiling water, ensuring the top millimetre or so is scalded, ie sterilized. Immediately lie a new, clean polythene bag over the pots and put them back on the tray in a safe place to cool down.

Two days after collecting the spores, and without opening the envelope, flick it with your fingers, and brown dust – hopefully, the spores – should be seen as a residue along the bottom of the envelope if it is held up to a bright light.

If you wish, the spores can now be cleaned, but I rarely bother and suggest for a first run it is not necessary. Clean spores by tapping the contents of the spore packet onto a clean sheet of paper in a room with no draughts. Hold the paper at 45 degrees and gently tap it so that all the larger pieces of debris fall away, leaving the spores in the grain of the paper. Fold the paper in half and tap more vigorously and the spores will drop into the crease. Sow the spores by gently tapping them onto the sterilized compost. Do this in a still room, ensuring all other pots are kept covered to avoid stray spores falling where they are not wanted. Label the pots and immediately put them inside the polythene bag on a tray. Fold the end of the bag under – in a few minutes condensation will appear on the polythene. Put the tray somewhere warm and forget it.

Depending on species and time of year, growth should be visible on the compost surface in two to six months. The initial growths are the prothalli. Periodically inspect the cultures and, in time, the first true leaves will appear. If after a year no true leaves are visible, the culture may have become too dry: spray cool boiled water onto the surface.

Once there is a good crop of true leaves, prick out little clumps (individual plants tend to die) into sterilized compost in seed trays. Water or spray gently with cool boiled water and put each tray in a polythene bag. Check fortnightly for moisture and growth. When you can see nice little plants, try leaving the neck of the bag open overnight, then gradually increase the air, eventually taking the bag off completely. Keep weaned plants out of the sun and well watered, but not waterlogged. Pot them up as necessary and eventually plant them out.

From leaf bases

Some ferns are sterile and do not produce spores; one of these, *Asplenium scolopendrium* Crispum Group, can be propagated from leaf bases – a surprisingly simple process. This can be done at any time of year but growth is obviously quicker in late spring or summer.

Select your plant, wash off all the soil and examine the rootstock. You will see a dead-looking caudex covered with equally dead-looking leaf bases. Using your thumbnail, push these downwards and they will snap away from the caudex leaving a green wound – proving there is life! Remove as many old leaf bases as required (putting them in a polythene bag), leaving green leaves in place. Repot the plant and nurse it carefully and it should recover fully. Wash the removed leaf bases, taking off any dead roots and shrivelled leaf remnants until you have a plump section 5–15mm (¼–⅜in) long.

Prepare a tray of sterilized compost or sand and plant the leaf bases, erect but upsidedown (green end upwards), in rows. Place the tray in a clean polythene bag and forget it for about two months. Examine the base tips with a hand lens and, with luck, you should see either translucent swellings, in effect bulbils, or the beginnings of green growth. Replace the tray in the polythene bag for six months to a year, by which time you should have little plants that can be hardened off gradually before potting up.

From bulbils

Other ferns, usually polystichums, produce bulbils along the rachis, and these usually assume the proportions of small plants within one growing season.

Bulbils along rachis of Polystichum setiferum *'Plumoso-multilobum'.*

The bulbils can be propagated by simply pegging the frond down onto good compost while it is still on the plant, or by removing it and doing the same thing in the potting shed. Prepare trays of peat (sterilization is not essential), make a groove in the compost and lay the section of the frond with the bulbils into it so that the bulbils are on the upper surface. Fix it in place with a sprinkle of grit on the leafy part of the frond, not on the bulbils, at the same time firming the compost against the sides of the rachis, trying to ensure that the bulbils' bases are in contact with the compost. Water, and place the whole tray into a polythene bag. Leave it for a month or two; when new growth can be seen, gradually harden off as before, then pot up when well rooted.

I use peat to propagate bulbils because I want to starve them into producing roots. A rich compost tends to encourage a lot of foliage but insufficient roots.

Apospory

Apospory, where the fern bypasses the prothallial stage, is an uncommon phenomenon but useful horticulturally in propagating *Athyrium filix-femina* 'Clarissima'. The technique involves layering a frond as if it were bulbiferous. The only practical difference is that *A. filix-femina* is deciduous and, therefore, the tray must be kept frost free.

By division

Rhizomatous ferns, such as polypodiums, are usually propagated by cutting off sections of rhizome. This often means that there are relatively few of the particular ferns in cultivation, but those that are available are often the originals.

Normal clump-forming ferns can be split in the same way as many flowering plants; make sure you get the spade cleanly between each crown before making a cut.

Polypodium ×
mantoniae
'*Cornubiense*',
*is suitable for
propagating by
division.*

Pests and diseases

Fortunately, neither pests nor diseases are common with garden ferns grown in a mixed border. In a monoculture problems are more likely to arise, but all can be kept in check by good husbandry.

Pests

Slugs and snails can attack certain leathery species, such as *Asplenium fontanum*, but once mature most ferns are immune. Vine weevils are a serious menace in pot culture if allowed to get out of control, but they are well controlled by modern chemicals, such as imidacloprid. An alternative to using chemicals is biological control with the pathogenic nematode *Steinernema kraussei*. This should be watered into the pots in August before the vine weevil grubs have grown large enough to cause damage. The nematode is available from mail order suppliers of biological control. It is also advisable to squeeze the obnoxious white larvae whenever they are found. Similarly, if you see an adult – squash it! Vine weevils in the garden rarely seem to do any damage to ferns.

In late summer in the garden you may notice the spore-bearing areas of fronds have gone brown, even on the upper surfaces of the fronds. This is almost certainly moth larvae eating the sori, and can cause some minor disfigurement but otherwise does no real harm and is not worth spraying. Rare in gardens, but common in the wild, is a fly larva that eats out the frond's growing point causing pseudo-cresting, usually in *Athyrium filix-femina*. Not beautiful, it is best controlled by picking off the distorted frond tips.

This close-up of the underside of a frond of Dryopteris × complexa *'Stablerae' (crisped) shows where a moth larva has grazed on the leaf tissues.*

DISEASES

There are two main fungal diseases of ferns: *Taphrina wettsteiniana* on polystichums and *Milesina scolopendrii* on *Asplenium scolopendrium*.

Taphrina wettsteiniana is a disfiguring disease related to peach leaf curl. Both are difficult to control. Taphrina causes masses of dark brown blotches, particularly towards the base of the frond after wet weather, and some frond distortion. The lesions may only be one or two millimetres across, but examine the frond with a hand lens during active growth immediately after wet weather and you may be able to see a silvery sheen of spores around the margin.

Taphrinas are biotrophic diseases, spread by rain, and they can be suppressed by drenching the plant's crown with a systemic fungicide. I recommend removing all diseased leaves or parts of leaves as well. The plant will recover in the following year, although it is a good idea to give it another fungicide drench in early spring. When watering, try to avoid applying unnecessary water to the foliage as this can encourage the disease.

If the disease is really severe on a particular plant, as a last resort you can bring it under cover for a season or two to prevent the foliage from getting wet. I did this with an extremely rare cultivar which I thought I was going to lose, and it is fine again now. Because the disease is distributed by rain-

Above: Polystichum setiferum 'Plumosum Bevis' with frond browning and distortion caused by Taphrina wettsteiniana.

Left: Dryopteris × complexa 'Stablerae' (crisped) showing insect damage.

splash, it is slow to spread from plant to plant unless the plants are very close together.

Milesina scolopendrii appears as brown blotches, perhaps 2.5cm (1in) across, on the leaves. Although this is a rust disease, the spores are white and can be seen quite easily on the underside of lesions when they are active. Like Taphrina, this is spread by wet weather. For control, remove diseased fronds and avoid watering the fronds unnecessarily. This disease is rarely as damaging as Taphrina and it can be suppressed with a systemic fungicide.

Below: Polystichum setiferum *'Plumoso-multilobum' after attack by Taphrina; the infected fronds have been removed.*

Leaf blotching

Above right: Asplenium scolopendrium *'Bolton's Nobile' with lesions caused by* Milesina scolopendrii *on the fronds.*

If ferns are allowed to remain too wet the fronds can blacken prematurely. This usually seems to be a physiological state that can be controlled by maintaining good air flow. I find it useful to remove autumn leaf fall from the crowns of hardy ferns and from around the base of rhizomatous ferns such as polypodiums.

FERNS IN THE GARDEN

COMPANIONS

As a fern grower I find that other plants in fern borders are not a priority, and I feel it is largely a matter of taste what to grow with them. However, I consider the following pleasant companions for my ferns.

Snowdrops – although they get a bit leafy and untidy in late spring. Other bulbs, such as *Erythronium*, *Narcissus*, *Leucojum*, are also effective.

Cyclamen, especially with *Polypodium*.

Arisaemas, especially *A. candidissimum*.

Roscoea cautleoides.

Hellebores – again the foliage can be a bit too abundant.

Primulas, especially the candelabra types.

Any **shrubs** with open foliage, such as *Acer japonicum* cultivars and *Hamamelis*.

Gunnera manicata, especially with osmundas.

Grasses, such as *Molinia caerulea* 'Strahlenquelle', *Hakonechloa macra* 'Aureola' and sedges, such as *Carex pendula*.

Ivies – I avoid because they eventually swamp the ferns.

Hostas.

Ferns (Polystichum munitum) and grasses (Molinia caerulea 'Strahlenquelle') making a splendid semi-formal bed at RHS Garden Rosemoor in Devon.

STUMPERIES AND ROCKERIES

Stumperies are a wonderful way to set off ferns. I find gnarled pieces of wood the ideal foil for displaying ferns at flower shows – suitable pieces of wood often turn up in my garden after a gale and are thus freely available. The concept can be transferred easily to the garden. Wood can be laid between plants and can even be used to dramatic effect by the selection of large pieces or stumps to dominate a border. The Patron of the British Pteridological Society, HRH The Prince of Wales, has created a wonderful stumpery in his garden at Highgrove in Gloucestershire. Another stumpery, more readily accessible, can be seen in the National Trust garden at Biddulph Grange, near Stoke-on-Trent in Staffordshire.

Rockeries work in much the same way as stumperies, but they are more difficult and usually more expensive to create. Fern roots love cool, moist soil, and therefore do well planted beside a rock or a stump. Both can also provide valuable overwinter protection for slightly tender species.

Rickard's Hardy Ferns display at the RHS Flower Show at Tatton Park, Cheshire, where the use of wood in a type of stumpery helps to show off the ferns.

Dicksonia antarctica protected with polystyrene for the winter.

LANDSCAPING

Many of the ferns commonly available commercially are those that are easiest to grow and most popular with the public. These are also the best plants for landscaping: they do well in a wide range of conditions and are best able to survive a fair amount of neglect. There are other species that would do well in these situations, but they are usually less easily propagated and therefore rarer. Most rare species are not suitable for general landscaping because they need more tender loving care than is practical. Rare ferns, such as *Polystichum setiferum* 'Plumosum Green', 'Gracillimum' or *Athyrium filix-femina* 'Clarissima', are often even more beautiful than the commoner types, but they can be expensive and are best confined to smaller garden or the specialist collection.

TREE FERNS

In recent years tree ferns, especially *Dicksonia antarctica*, have become available and much sought after by keen growers. They have proved unexpectedly easy to grow throughout lowland Britain and much of Europe. They are rarely available in the USA so as yet we do not know how they will do there, but I would expect them to thrive in zone 9 or warmer as long as there is plentiful moisture.

Tree ferns can be bought at any time of the year, but it is easiest to buy them in spring and early summer as logs – that is, without fronds or visible roots. They are often cheaper in this form, and they are certainly much easier to transport. By late summer they need to be fronding up so that fronds can harden off before frosts arrive. Late-season fronds always disappear with the first frost. During the first season there is often very little root production so do not be alarmed if a recently bought specimen falls out of its pot! Repot it and root growth will eventually make it stable. Curiously, root growth seems to be quicker over winter.

Care

The following procedure works well for *Dicksonia antarctica*:

If the log is less than 60cm (2ft) tall, do not risk it outside over winter in zone 9 – it might survive but the risks are too great; in zone 10 it should be fine. Trunks of more than 60cm can be left outside with protection in zone 9. In many cases, fat trunks are better than thin ones as they have greater in-built insulation against cold and are less prone to dry out. Thin trunks look more elegant, however, but avoid very slim ones, say less than 10cm (4in) in diameter, for outside in zone 9.

When you get your log home, soak the bottom 30–60cm (12–24in) of trunk for 10 minutes or so; do not wet the crown. Plant at least 5cm (2in) of trunk per 30cm of total length – that is plant 10cm of a 60cm trunk or 30cm of a 1.8m (6ft) trunk. This is the minimum amount and is just enough to hold the plant steady. If you are unable to give the plant plenty of love and a daily watering, plant it deeper, giving the trunk a greater interface with the soil and so greater potential for obtaining some water by itself.

Watering is critical. *D. antarctica* always grows well if it is well watered. For the first year, assume the plant is not getting much water from the soil, and water it daily. In a large garden or park site, consider irrigation to the trunk. In the first year water copiously daily from about 15cm (6in) below the crown, right down to the base and all around – back and front. In the second year water like this every second day, the third year every third day, and after that as necessary. In a damp, shady spot the fern can survive without any water, year in, year out, once established. I never recommend watering in the crown for fear of initiating rotting. In the height of summer it is probably acceptable but it is not a good habit to get into.

Over winter in Zone 10 or colder, play safe and protect the crown with a layer of straw about 15cm (6in) thick, firmed deep into the crown. This is adequate down to −10°C (14°F) but for extra security you can invert a plastic or metal plate over the straw to keep it drier, it might also be worth wrapping the top 45cm (18in) of trunk in hessian. I favour hessian because it is a similar colour to the trunk and therefore not such an eyesore as fleece or polystyrene. I avoid bubblewrap in case it leads to undue sweating in the crown, which may lead to rotting. The bottom part of the trunk is left open to the elements and makes some watering possible in mild spells after a long dry period. The aim of this whole process is to prevent the crown from freezing. The drier the straw, the better; if it is dry, ice cannot form.

Quite a few species of tree fern are becoming available in Europe. *Dicksonia antarctica* is almost certainly the hardiest. In zone 9 you could also try *D. fibrosa* and *Cyathea australis*, but neither is as easy as *D. antarctica*. In zone 10 *D. squarrosa*, *C. dealbata*, *C. cooperi*, *C. medullaris* and *C. smithii* are all worth a try with protection. Larger plants have a better chance of survival as long as they are treated as outlined for *Dicksonia antarctica*.

The entire trunk of Cyathea australis protected for the winter with hessian.

FERN SPECIES AND CULTIVARS

This section features, in alphabetical order, the most widely grown ferns and their species and cultivars. A description of each genus, usually defining the main generic characteristics, is followed by information on the most important species. Among the details provided initially are common names, the natural range of the species, height and cultivation requirements (**abbreviations are explained in the key, below**). Each entry then gives distinguishing characters for the species and a range of cultivars as appropriate. Cultivars follow their parent species in whether they are deciduous or evergreen; size, hardiness and soil preferences are also similar to the parent's, unless additionally given.

Key

H = height or frond length.

D = deciduous.

E = evergreen.

W = wintergreen
(usually ferns that die down in summer).

Moisture requirements: dry = exposed and sunny, usually among stones, dry–wet = on the dry side, typically a normal, moist, but not wet, shady border, often under trees; wet–dry = on the wet side, a wet shady border; wet = very wet conditions, usually boggy or waterside.

Zone = hardiness of the fern, calculated using the system devised by the US Department of Agriculture (see p. 38).

Dryopteris cycadina.

Hardiness zones

Temperatures given are the average annual minimum temperatures. Over the last 22 years in our central England location, we have fluctuated between zone 5 and zone 9, but we are usually in zone 8, which I have taken as the local rating; when we get a zone 5 winter we must expect problems. The zones are calculated as follows:

Zone	Temperature (°C)	Temperature (°F)
1	below –46°C	(below –50°F)
2	–46 to –40°C	(–50 to –40°F)
3	–40 to –34°C	(–40 to –30°F)
4	–34 to –29°C	(–30 to –20°F)
5	–29 to –23°C	(–20 to –10°F)
6	–23 to –18°C	(–10 to 0°F)
7	–18 to –12°C	(0 to 10°F)
8	–12 to –7°C	(10 to 20°F)
9	–7 to –1°C	(20 to 30°F)
10	–1 to 4°C	(30 to 40°F)
11	above 4°C	(above 40°F)

Deciduous or evergreen?

Unfortunately, deciduous ferns are often overlooked in favour of evergreen ones; to me, both are equally attractive: evergreen ferns can be enjoyed virtually all year, but the sudden emergence of the spring flush of growth of deciduous ferns such as the lady fern takes some beating.

Adiantum (Maidenhair ferns)

Around the world there are many species and cultivars of *Adiantum*. Most are tender and only suitable for a conservatory or as house plants. A few, however, are wonderful fully hardy species that deserve to be widely grown in gardens in Britain and other cool, temperate parts of the world. Maidenhair ferns are very distinctive and beautiful with thin shiny black petioles and green, fan-shaped pinnules; the spores are produced at intervals under the folded-back edge of the pinnule.

Above: Adiantum aleuticum *at Sizergh Castle, Cumbria.*

Right: Adiantum aleuticum *'Imbricatum'.*

A. aleuticum (Aleutian maidenhair) AGM Western North America, H30–60cm (12–24in), D, dry–wet, zone 3. Only recently recognized as distinct from the very similar *A. pedatum*. Both have upright fronds divided into bipinnate, pedate (fan-shaped) lamina with fan-shaped pinnules. In *A. aleuticum* the pinnules are smaller and often slightly curled. It can be tricky to establish: plant out of the wind in moist but not very wet soil; pH is not an issue. Young foliage can be red-tinted but never as brightly as in 'Japonicum'. **'Imbricatum'** Western North America, H15–30cm (6–12in), D, dry–wet. Like the species but smaller, not the true dwarf (see 'Subpumilum'). **'Japonicum'** (Japanese maidenhair) Japan. Differs in having beautiful red foliage in spring. It eventually turns green, although mid- to late- season fronds are also colourful. It is also less reliable, and may be less hardy, than the parent species, but its stunning beauty makes it worth a try. **'Subpumilum'** (Dwarf maidenhair) AGM British Columbia, H5–10cm (2–4in), D but E in mild winters. A wonderful compact dwarf form, uncommon in cultivation and worth looking for.

A. capillus-veneris (True maidenhair)
Much of the tropical and temperate
world, including Southwest Britain,
H30–38cm (12–15in), D, dry–wet,
zone 9, possibly 8. Fronds narrowly
triangular, bipinnate to tripinnate. Sori
elongate along the pinnule margin, not
circular. Its hybrid with an unknown
species in cultivation, known as *A.* ×
mairisii AGM, is larger and hardy, and a
reliable good doer. It is rarely available
as I understand that it can only be
propagated by division. Good drifts of
it can be seen at Barnard Green House,
Great Malvern, Worcestershire.

Above: Adiantum ×
mairisii *at Barnard
Green House.*

A. pedatum (Eastern maidenhair) AGM Eastern North America,
H45–60cm (18–24in), D, dry–wet, zone 3. A beautiful fern very
similar to *A. aleuticum*. Plants in cultivation as 'Miss Sharples' are
probably this species.

A. venustum (Himalayan
maidenhair) AGM Central Asia,
H23–38cm (9–15in), D but E in mild
winters, dry, zone 5. Fronds tripinnate
and narrowly deltate. Probably the
best of all the garden maidenhairs;
once established it will grow to form
large clumps, and it divides easily.
Unfortunately, it is very slow from
spores and therefore rarely available
commercially.

Asplenium (Spleenworts, hart's tongue ferns)

The spleenworts are a large group of
small ferns with many species hardy in
zone 9 or colder. They have a delicate

Adiantum
venustum.

beauty that can enhance rockwork or stone troughs, but are sometimes
difficult to establish. The hart's tongues (*A. scolopendium*) are larger with
strap-shaped fronds and are good robust garden plants. Sori linear.

A. *ceterach* (syn. *Ceterach officinarum;* **Rusty back fern**) North-west Europe, including Britain, H8–20cm (3–8in), E, dry, zone 5. This beautiful fern has pinnatifid fronds with triangular lobes, and the underside is densely covered with brown scales. It is very rarely sold commercially and difficult to grow, but appears in many fern lists. It is best grown in a very stony, calcareous, free-draining mix – the soil on the top of a crumbling dry stone wall is ideal. In dry weather the fronds curl up, reopening in moist weather.

Asplenium
ceterach.

A. *dareoides* Chile, H8–20cm (3–8in), E, dry–wet, zone 5. Fronds tripinnate, roundly triangular with rounded pinnules. A very attractive creeping fern well suited to a well-drained rock garden. It grows naturally as an epiphyte on trees.

A. *fontanum* (**Fountain spleenwort**) Central Europe, H8–30cm (3–12in), E, dry–wet, zone 5. Fronds bipinnate, lance-shaped with virtually no stalk because the pinnae are produced from very near the frond base. Likes calcareous, rocky soil with good drainage but beware of slug damage.

A. *scolopendrium* (syn. *Phyllitis scolopendrium;* **hart's tongue**) AGM Europe, including Britain, H45–60cm (18–24in), E, dry–wet, zone 5. Fronds entire, strap-shaped, a very familiar fern in Southwest England and a wonderful garden plant. Any planting of ferns should include some hart's tongues as they contrast so beautifully with the archetypal filigree ferns. Limey soil is preferred but not essential, although plants can lack vigour on very acid, sandy soils. Too much sun can burn the fronds, especially of the thinner-textured crispums. May suffer from *Milesina scolopendrii,* see p.29. Many cultivars have been named in the past, and quite a few are still in cultivation. The following are available commercially: **Crispum Group** These have thinner-textured fronds, no sori and deeply crisped frond margins, which fold back on themselves in the style of an Elizabethan ruff. Propagation is vegetative, either by division of the crowns or by rooting leaf bases, see pp.22–25. No crispums are common, but **'Crispum Bolton's Nobile'** AGM is very occasionally available. It is a beautiful, broad-fronded form, up to 10cm (4in) wide. Another rarer type is **'Golden Queen'**, which is similar to 'Bolton's Nobile' but has the additional character of streaks of yellow running from the midrib to the margin,

Above: Asplenium scolopendrium *'Ramo-cristatum'*.

Left: Asplenium scolopendrium *'Crispum Bolton's Nobile'*.

making it particularly susceptible to over-exposure to midday sun: plant in dappled shade. **'Cristatum'** Fronds crested towards tip. In some selections the crest can be small and neat, while in others the frond can branch repeatedly. If the branching occurs in the lower half of the frond the cultivar is more precisely termed **'Ramo-cristatum'**. **Fimbriatum Group** H30cm (12in). Fronds fairly stiff, narrow with serrated margins. Very pretty. **'Laceratum Kaye'** (or **'Kaye's Lacerated'**) AGM H20–30cm (8–12in). Fronds lax, broad, with deeply lacerated margins. Spore grown plants are slightly variable but fronds usually broadest at base. A chance sporeling at Reginald Kaye's nursery around 1952. **'Marginatum'** Very similar to Fimbriatum Group but has the added feature of one or two wings of tissue running the entire length on the underside of the frond. Rarely available commercially but is occasionally seen in the wild. **'Muricatum'** Similar to the species except that the upper surface of the frond is covered with little pimples, particularly near the midrib. Not a great beauty, nor commonly available but can turn up in wild populations. **Ramo-marginatum Group** H20–30cm (8–12in) Fronds brittle, erect, dark green, branched from the base, not usually crested. Each frond branch has an irregular margin.

Ideal where a smaller evergreen fern is needed, especially in a trough. **Undulatum Group** Similar to Crispum Group but differs in that it bears spores. To the purist this is not as good as Crispum but the general gardener might not notice the difference. When young, the two forms are difficult to separate but Undulatum Group becomes less undulate when spores are produced. A good proportion of Undulatum progeny fail to produce spores even at maturity, and become Crispum by default – a happy occurrence!

A. trichomanes (**Maidenhair spleenwort**) AGM Cosmopolitan, including Britain, H8–20cm (3–8in), E, dry–wet, zone 3. A pretty little fern with simple pinnate fronds rarely more than 2.5cm (1in) wide.

Pinnae are round or short oblong on a shiny black or brown midrib. The commercial form is **subsp.** *quadrivalens*, which likes lime; it is equally well suited to borders, rock gardens or stone troughs. '**Incisum Moule**' Differs in having deeply incised pinnae margins. '**Ramocristatum**'[16] Similar to species except that the frond branches near the base and each section is crested at its tip. '**Cristatum**' is similar but uncommon; the fronds are crested but unbranched. '**Stuart Williams**' A very attractive crested sport of 'Incisum Moule' named after the well-known RHS judge who first raised it.

Asplenium trichomanes 'Incisum Moule'.

Athyrium (Lady ferns)

Deciduous ferns for shady moist borders. Spores are borne on the backs of the fronds in linear or J-shaped indusia. As a group they are tough plants with a delicate, rather feminine appearance, hence the common name.

A. × '**Branford Beauty**' North America, H45cm (18in), D, wet–dry, zone 6. Presumed to be a hybrid with one parent being *A. niponicum* var. *pictum* – it differs from this by being slightly less colourful and having suberect fronds. The other parent is not known for sure but it is probably an American native species. Propagate by division or tissue culture.

A. × '**Branford Rambler**' North America, H30cm (12in), D, wet–dry, zone 6. Similar to 'Branford Beauty' but slightly less colourful again, shorter and spreads more rapidly, but not invasive in my experience. Again presumed to be a hybrid between *A. niponicum* var. *pictum* and a native North American species. Propagate by division or tissue culture.

A. × **'Ghost'** North America, H50–75cm (20–30in), D, wet–dry, zone 6. Fronds erect, grey, retaining a little of the purple of the parent species along the midrib. Occurred as a chance hybrid in Nancy Swell's garden in Richmond, Virginia, USA. One parent is presumed to be *A. niponicum* and the other a native North American species. To my mind it is one of the most exciting introductions in recent years. When I first saw it in a New York garden. I was stopped in my tracks. I had never seen such a magnificent grey or silvery hardy specimen fern before. Note the small size of *A. niponicum* growing beside 'Ghost' in the photograph. Propagate by division or tissue culture although it may be partially fertile.

Athyrium ×
'Ghost'.

A. angustatum f. *rubellum* **'Lady in Red'** North America, 50–75cm (24–30in), D, wet–dry, zone 6. The species *A. angustatum* differs little from *A. filix-femina,* but this wonderful form has a vibrant burgundy rachis and midrib. It was found growing wild in the north-east USA during a field trip of a local botanical society. All plants distributed under this name are propagated by tissue culture and are therefore identical.

A. filix-femina **(Lady fern)** AGM Northern hemisphere, including Britain, H1–1.5m (3–5ft), D, wet, zone 3. Very common in moist sites through most of its range. Fronds tripinnate, lance-shaped with a short stipe. Grows in sunny spots if well supplied with water, although sun-grown plants are usually less finely dissected (less feathery). Lady fern is one of the easiest species to raise from spores, but unfortunately the cultivars rarely come true; hence it is often incorrect to call sporelings after the clone name, such as 'Cristatum', and better to use the more general name, such as Cristatum Group. If any raised plants are of

special merit they might eventually be selected and named in their own right. Due to their smaller size and tougher texture some dwarf cultivars, such as Congestum Group and 'Frizelliae', can withstand a drier, more open spot in the garden than the larger, leafier lady ferns. Over 300 cultivars have been described; the following are most likely to be met in cultivation: **'Clarissimum'** This is grown as two forms, one named after Jones, the other after Bolton. They are very similar: both have tall, broad tripinnate forms, and the space between the ultimate segments is much wider than in the species, giving a very airy appearance. It is one of the most beautiful of all ferns, but sadly both clones are very rare and sell at around £350 each; occasional aposporous forms are available commercially much more cheaply, although not quite so good. A sterile form, only propagated by division or by apospory (see p.25). **Cristatum Group** Crested at the frond and pinnae tip, the terminal crest more or less flat in the plane of the frond. Other closely related forms include **'Capitatum'**, where only the tip of the frond is crested, not the pinnae; **'Corymbiferum'**, where the crest is three-dimensional (that is, bunched in several planes); **'Grandiceps'**, where the terminal crest is broader than the frond and **'Percristatum'** where the pinnulets are crested. **Congestum Group** H20–40cm (8–16in). A small, neat plant with the rachis and pinnae midribs reduced in length and texture of frond thicker than in the species, somewhat brittle. More often found crested, then named **'Congestum Cristatum'**. **Cruciatum Group** Pinnae fork at the point of attachment to the rachis; where pinnae are opposite each other a cross is formed, then repeated many times up the rachis; tips of pinnae and frond are both crested. A very unusual and attractive form. These plants are often referred to collectively as **'Victoriae'**, but none in general nursery trade is a true 'Victoriae', which is a very rare cultivar that may cost £250, with cross-shaped pinnules and narrow ultimate divisions with a green rachis. The nursery trade plants are usually sporelings of 'Victoriae', often several generations removed and nowhere near as striking. **'Lady Victoria'** is a new cruciate clone propagated by tissue culture. Not true 'Victoriae' but very close and well worth growing. **'Fieldii'** is another old named clone sometimes on offer; again, it is unlikely to be the original clone. It differs from the Victoriae Group by being more leafy. **'Frizelliae' (Tatting fern)** AGM H15–25cm (6–10in) Frond pinnate, pinnae reduced to tiny shell-like lobes along each side of the rachis, said to resemble lace (tatting). Forms of the size specified can be found in general cultivation, but many plants are taller, with shell-like pinnae erratically replaced by simple or forking pinnae. In batches of sporelings, forms

Athyrium filix-femina *'Frizelliae'*.

with branching fronds (Frizelliae Ramosum Group) and crested fronds (Frizelliae Cristatum Group) are not uncommon. **'Minutissimum'** H30–60cm (12–24in) Not one of my favourites – formerly quite widely grown, quite uncommon now. The fronds are usually not small enough to deserve the cultivar name. **Plumosum Group** Fronds tri-, quadri- or even quinquepinnate, very lacy and feathery – a beautiful group. On the face of it similar to *'Clarissima'* but most plumosums are fertile. They do not come absolutely true from spores, but all progeny are worth keeping. The named form most often encountered, but never common, is

Close up of Athyrium filix-femina 'Setigerum Cruciatum'.

'Plumosum Axminster' with tri- or, in well-grown specimens, quadripinnate fronds. There are several other cultivars, including **Plumosum Cristatum Group**, which differ subtly from each other; although none are usually available commercially, they are all worth looking out for. **'Setigerum'** Like the species except the pinnule tips are bristly. Can hybridize with other cultivars, to give, for example, **Setigerum Congestum Group** or **Setigerum Cruciatum Group** or

Setigerum Cristatum Group. **'Vernoniae'** AGM Fronds as the species except the basal pinnules are on short stipes; all pinnules are crispy and elliptical with lacerated margins. In spore sowings **'Vernoniae Cristatum'** is not uncommon.

***A. niponicum* var. *pictum* (syn. *A. goeringianum* 'Picton')** AGM Japan, H20–40cm (8–16in), D, wet–dry, zone 6. Quite rightly one of the most popular garden ferns, with fronds bipinnate, lance-shaped, spreading (rarely erect) and a mixture of purple, grey and green. If grown too dry, it tends to languish; prefers a moist, shady spot but not where it might get flooded. I succeeded well with this where it was planted at the base of a stone in a shady rockery. Offspring from spores can vary in the colour intensity, with some lacking purple altogether. Most strains are good, however, and even the green form is pretty and worth growing. Crested forms crop up from time to time; they are very attractive and can be improved by selective breeding. **'Silver Falls'** is a recently introduced selection with strong colouring.

Athyrium filix-femina Plumosum Cristatum Group.

A. otophorum (**Eared lady fern**) AGM Japan, H30–45 (12–18in), D, wet–dry, zone 5. Fronds bipinnate, lance-shaped; stipes and pinna midribs red; lamina green. In spring the new fronds are a very striking bright yellow/green for a short while. Fronds persist into autumn longer than those of other lady ferns.

A. vidalii Japan, H30–45cm (12–18in), D, wet–dry, zone 6. Fronds bipinnate, lance-shaped with reddish midribs. New fronds reddish but not as colourful as *A. otophorum* or the *A. niponicum* section of plants.

Blechnum (**Hard ferns**)

A large genus of usually dimorphic ferns, producing two types of lance-shaped, pinnate or pinnatifid fronds: vegetative fronds with broad pinnae and held between the horizontal and 45 degrees, and fertile fronds with narrow pinnae and held more or less upright. This creates a very pleasing structure, the ring of spreading fronds forming a halo of foliage around the more wiry, upright sporing fronds. The edge of the pinna of the sporing fronds is rolled under to form the indusium protecting the sporangia; the linear sori are borne along both sides of the pinnae under the rolled-under margin. Early in the season many blechnums produce very attractive pink or sometimes yellow foliage that eventually turns green. Unfortunately, blechnums dislike lime, and can, therefore, only be considered for neutral to acid gardens.

Blechnum chilense flushing mainly red fronds in the Chilean wilderness during springtime.

B. chilense AGM Chile, H1–1.5m (3–5ft), E, wet–dry, zone 7. Fronds pinnate, up to 23cm (9in) wide, dark green but often red when young. Lamina uneven, not glossy. In time produces narrow creeping stolons that spread to form clumps. Propagation is usually from these runners. Occasionally a well-established crown can develop a rhizome with a short trunk, usually less than 15cm (6in), but in Chile I have seen slender trunks over 30cm (12in) tall and 10cm (4in) wide. Often incorrectly grown as *B. tabulare* or *B. magellanicum*.

B. discolor New Zealand, H40cm (16in), W, wet–dry, zone 8–9. Fronds pinnatifid, 5–8cm (2–3in) wide, dull pale green, almost white underneath. Trunk-forming; seems hardy but can suffer in a cold snap.

B. fluviatile New Zealand, Australia, H45cm (18in), E, wet–dry, zone 6. Fronds pinnate, 3–5cm (1¼–2in) wide, dull green, rachis conspicuously scaly. Very pretty, can produce a slender trunk up to 30cm (12in) tall in its native rainforests.

Athyrium otophorum.

B. magellanicum Chile, H30cm–2.4m (1–8ft), E, wet–dry, zone 6. There can be few hardy ferns to match the drama of this overlooked species. I have recently had the great pleasure of seeing it in the wilds of Chile: it is a beauty! The fronds can grow to 1.5m (5ft) long, and it can produce a trunk up to 1.5m (5ft) tall by 30cm (12in) wide – a tree fern in every sense, except that it is not a member of the true tree fern family. The pinnae are smooth, glossy and pointed. Because of its trunk, a mature specimen cannot be confused with any other fern, but young plants are not so easy: they can be separated from young *B. chilense* because their pinnae are not stalked – it is really pinnatifid where *B. chilense* is pinnate (that is, it has stalked pinnae). I have not heard of this being grown in the northern hemisphere but it should be very hardy; in the Andes *B. chilense* is common at low altitude,s but by about 800m (2,650ft) in central Chile it dies out, to be replaced by *B. magellanicum*.

B. novae-zelandiae New Zealand, H60cm–1.5m (2–5ft), W, wet–dry, zone 7. Fronds pinnatifid, 15–23cm (6–9in) wide, yellow-green when mature, yellow or sometimes pink when young. Can produce a stubby trunk.

B. nudum Australia, H60cm (2ft), E, wet–dry, zone 9. Fronds pinnatifid, 10–15cm (4–6in) wide, always green, never coloured when young. Usually produces a trunk, making it a very handsome dwarf tree fern. Trunked specimens may not be reliably hardy in zone 9, hence probably best in a conservatory over winter.

B. penna-marina AGM Temperate southern hemisphere, H8–23cm (3–9in), E, wet–dry, zone 5. Fronds pinnatifid, dark green, 1cm (½in) wide. Rhizome creeping, eventually giving delightful evergreen groundcover. Fertile fronds longer than vegetative fronds. Some forms have red foliage in spring.

B. spicant AGM Temperate northern hemisphere, including Britain, H30–45cm (12–18in), E, wet–dry, zone 4. Fronds pinnatifid, dark green, 3cm (1¼in) wide. A common British wild species and an excellent garden plant.

B. tabulare South Africa, H30cm–1.2m (1–4ft), E, wet–dry, zone 10. Probably not hardy in any but the most protected British gardens, but included here because it is often confused with *B. chilense. B. tabulare* is a trunk-forming species, very similar to *B. magellanicum*, from which it differs in not having pointed pinnae tips. I have seen this on the summit of Table Mountain in South Africa.

Cheilanthes (Lip ferns)

A large genus of ferns adapted to drier parts of the world, growing among rocks where humidity may linger. Usually covered with scales or hairs to slow water loss; in very dry weather the fronds normally

The upright sporing fronds are distinctive in Blechnum spicant.

curl up to slow it further. Most lip ferns are hardy in zone 9 in an unheated, well-ventilated cold greenhouse, but only a few are hardy in zone 9 gardens, and even then some skill is helpful to ensure their survival. (*Pellaea*, which is not included in this book, is similar in cultivation requirements.) The species described is forgiving of some neglect if appropriately sited. Sori under the rolled-up margin of the pinnae.

C. tomentosa South-east USA, H30–45cm (12–18in), E, dry, zone 6. Fronds lance-shaped, tripinnate with hairs making them an attractive grey-green colour, particularly on the underside. Plant in a well-drained, well-ventilated site with a liberal supply of grit. Overwinter the crowns of young plants under straw.

Cryptogramma (Parsley ferns)

Beautiful ferns, resembling parsley but sadly almost impossible to grow in gardens: they need acid soil and good drainage but high rainfall. All species are dimorphic, with tri- to quadripinnate lance-shaped fronds; as in *Blechnum* the segments of the sporing fronds are narrower. Fertile fronds are taller than vegetative fronds. Sori under margin of pinnae.

C. crispa (**Parsley fern**) Europe, including Britain, Asia, H8–30cm (3–12in), D, dry–wet, zone 2. Rarely available commercially but very common in the English Lake District.

Cyathea (Tree ferns)

A very large genus of tree ferns, generally less hardy than the other main tree fern genus – *Dicksonia*. The two genera are easily distinguished: *Cyathea* is scaly on the stipe and particularly in the crown and on the young unfurling croziers, while in *Dicksonia* the scales are replaced by hairs. Fronds generally have quite a long stipe and are broadly lance-shaped, almost triangular. At least one species, *C. australis*, is hardy in zone 9 if it is a good-sized specimen and given overwinter protection. Other species are becoming more widely available, but they are best considered less hardy until more widespread feedback on successes and failures in various areas is available. Sori naked, mid-distance between the pinnule midrib and its margin.

C. australis (**Rough tree fern**) Australia – Victoria, New South Wales, Tasmania. H trunk up to 5.5m (18ft) by 30cm (12in), fronds 1.2–3m (4–10ft), D, wet–dry, zone 9, possibly 8. Called the rough tree fern because the stipe is covered with short spines (it is wise to wear

Cheilanthes tomentosa.

gloves when lifting heavy specimens). Leaf bases obvious along top section of trunk, but lower down they are covered by mats of roots. Unlike most tree ferns *C. australis* likes good light; it is well-suited to more open sites than *Dicksonia antarctica*. Beware, plants offered in trade are often *C. cooperi*, a quick check for spine bases by rubbing the outside of the leaf base should confirm the identity.

C. brownii (**Norfolk Island tree fern**) Norfolk Island, H trunk to 3m (10ft) by 15cm (6in), fronds 1.2–2.5m (4–8ft), E, wet–dry, zone 10. Sometimes available as young plants, unlikely to be hardy in Britain. Difficult to distinguish from *C. cooperi* but has darker scales and a more leathery lamina.

C. cooperi (**Lacy tree fern**) Eastern Australia, H trunk to 2.5m (8ft) by 12cm (5in), fronds 1.2–2.5m (4–8ft), E, wet–dry, zone 9. Commonly available as young plants, but trunked specimens are rare; if available, the latter may be hardy in sheltered gardens.

C. dealbata (**Ponga, silver tree fern**) New Zealand, H trunk 6m (20ft) by 15cm (6in), fronds 1.2–2.5m (4–8ft), E, wet–dry, zone 9. Easily distinguished from all other tree ferns in general cultivation by the beautiful silver undersides of the fronds; young specimens, and those recently disturbed, may not show the silver for a season or two.

Cythea dealbata in Rosdohan garden, Co. Kerry, Ireland.

C. dregei South Africa, H trunk to 3.5m (12ft) by 45cm (18in), fronds 1.2–2.5m (4–8ft), D, wet–dry, zone 9, possibly 8. Could be as hardy as *C. australis* but trunked specimens are not available; young sporelings will need to be grown on for several years before meaningful hardiness testing can take place.

C. medullaris (**Black tree fern**) New Zealand, H trunk to 4.5m (15ft) (18m/60ft in the wild) by 10–23cm (4–9in), fronds 3m (10ft), E, wet–dry, zone 10, possibly 9. Stipe and rachis black on mature plants, green on sporelings. Possibly the most beautiful of all tree ferns but difficult until well-established; some success has been achieved in sheltered London gardens.

C. smithii (**Katote, soft tree fern**) New Zealand, H trunk 3m (10ft) by 30cm (12in), fronds 1.2–2m (4–6ft), E, wet–dry, zone 10. Stipe shorter and fronds narrower than the other species listed here: at a glance it looks more like a dicksonia. Despite growing in the wild further from the equator than any other tree fern, it does not seem to be one of the hardiest species.

C. tomentosissima Papua New Guinea, H trunk 1m (3ft) by 8cm (3in), fronds 1–1.5m (3–5ft), E, wet–dry, zone 10. Fronds lightly covered with orange-brown to pale brown scales which makes them appear hairy – hence tomentosissima.

Cyrtomium

A genus made up of several very similar species. Fronds oblong, pinnate with broad, entire, somewhat sickle-shaped pinnae. All are excellent garden plants, strongly recommended in mixed fern plantings as the frond texture contrasts beautifully with the more typical filigree fern foliage. Sori without an indusium scattered over the underside of the pinnae.

C. caryotideum Japan, east Asia, H45cm (18in), E, dry–wet, zone 7. Fronds pale green, spreading. Each pinna has a basal thumb. One of the most beautiful ferns in the genus.

C. falcatum (**Japanese holly fern**) AGM Japan, east Asia, H60cm (2ft), E, dry–wet, zone 8. Fronds dark green, glossy, some pinnae with a thumb. Reputed not to be terribly hardy, but it has done well with me for decades in zone 8. '**Rochfordianum**' is a good variant with deeply lacerated pinna margins.

C. fortunei AGM Japan, east Asia, H60cm (2ft), E, dry–wet, zone 6. Fronds erect, rather pale matt green. Pinnae narrower than other species with the margin smooth. **'Clivicola'** is similar but with broader pinnae and wavy margins on more spreading fronds.

C. lonchitoides Japan, east Asia, H45cm (18in), E, dry–wet, zone 6. Pinnae shorter and rounder than other species.

C. macrophyllum Japan, east Asia, H60cm (2ft), E, dry–wet, zone 7. Pinnae larger than in other species; it is most like *C. caryotideum* but differs in lacking a basal thumb on each pinna, and the fronds are darker green. Rarely available, but worth looking for as it is a beautiful fern.

Cystopteris (Bladder ferns)

A genus of delicate deciduous ferns, excellent for spring and summer effect but prone to browning-off in late summer. Sori bladder-shaped.

Cyrtomium macrophyllum.

C. bulbifera (**Bulblet bladder fern**) USA, H38cm (15in), D, dry–wet, zone 3. Fronds narrowly triangular, bipinnate, pale green. Bulbils are produced along the underside of the rachis and pinnae midribs. These fall off and soon produce a glut of young plants, which may become a nuisance, particularly in a rock garden.

C. dickieana (**Dickie's bladder fern**) Scotland, H10–15cm (4–6in), D, dry–wet, zone 4. Very pretty lance-shaped, bipinnate fronds. All segments are somewhat rounded and overlapping.

C. fragilis (**Brittle bladder fern**) Widespread in temperate zones, H15–20cm (6-8in), D, dry–wet, zone 2. Like *C. dickieana,* except pinnae not rounded and not tending to overlap each other. Common, but rarely grown because it dies back too soon; great for early spring effect.

C. tennesseensis (**Tennessee bladder fern**) USA, H30cm (12in), D, dry–wet, zone 5. Like *C. bulbifera*, but a fresher green and much more sparingly bulbiferous.

Cystopteris tennesseensis.

Davallia (Hare's foot ferns)

A medium-sized genus of beautiful ferns with triangular, usually tripinnate fronds produced on scaly creeping rhizomes. Sori shallowly tubular at the margin of the pinnules.

D. *mariesii* (Hardy hare's foot fern) AGM Japan, H23cm (9in), D, dry–wet, zone 8. Rhizome runs on or near the soil surface, soon growing into a colony. Very beautiful but slow in colder areas. Super in a hanging basket.

Dennstaedtia

A small genus of creeping ferns related to braken. Sori cup-shaped.

D. *punctiloba* (American hay-scented fern) USA, H60–90cm (2-3ft), D, wet–dry, zone 5. Neutral to acid soil only. Hairy, bipinnate fronds with a longish stipe and lance-shaped blades are produced at intervals on a creeping rhizome. Can be invasive and looks untidy by autumn, but gives good groundcover in a larger garden.

Deparia

A small genus of deciduous ferns, related to *Athyrium* and with linear sori.

D. *pycnosora* Asia, H30cm (12in), D, dry–wet, zone 8 or possibly colder. Fronds lance-shaped, pinnate-pinnatifid, pale green with white scales, especially on the rachis. I have not overwintered this fern in Britain but I have seen it in John Mickel's New York State garden where it survives cold winters.

Dicksonia (Tree ferns)

A small genus of 20–30 species, most forming a trunk. Differs from *Cyathea*, the other main genus of tree ferns by being hairy rather than scaly. Sori cup-shaped along margins of pinnulets.

D. antarctica (**Soft tree fern**) AGM Australia, H trunk to 6m (20ft) by 75cm (30in), fronds 1.2–2.5m (4–8ft) by 75cm, E to -8°C (18°F), wet–dry, zone 9, 8 with protection. Almost certainly the hardiest true tree fern. Fronds bipinnate, rachis covered with purplish hairs when young, stipe short or sometimes absent. Pinnae with margins turned down. Hairs in crown mid- to dark brown. A beautiful plant with stunning impact in the garden.

Dicksonia antarctica at RHS Garden Rosemoor in Devon.

D. fibrosa (**Wheki ponga**) AGM New Zealand, H trunk to 5.5m (18ft) by 60cm (2ft), fronds 1.2–2.5m (4–8ft) by 75cm (30in) but usually less in cultivation, E to -10°C (14°F), wet–dry, zone 9, possibly 8. Very similar to *D. antarctica*, but has a more fibrous trunk, pinnae with turned up edges and smaller darker fronds with a more conspicuously brown rachis. Hairs in crown dark brown. The turned-up pinnae edges are the best distinguishing feature: if you gently run your hand over the upper surfaces of the fronds of both species, *D. fibrosa* feels rough, while *D. antarctica* feels smooth. Because it is usually a smaller plant, *D. fibrosa* is better suited to conservatories.

D. sellowiana Brazil and northern South America, H to 3m (10ft) by 30cm (1ft), fronds 1.8–2.5m (6–8ft) by 60cm (2ft), E, wet–dry, zone 9. Almost impossible distinguish from *D. antarctica* except for having yellow-brown hairs in the crown. Usually only available as sporelings. One large plant in Hereford, England (zone 8), is growing very well with protection – apparently at least as hardy as *D. antarctica*.

D. squarrosa (**Wheki, rough tree fern**) New Zealand, H trunk to 3m (10ft) by 8–12cm (3–5in), fronds 1.2–2m (4–6ft) by 45cm (18in), E, wet–dry, zone 10. Fronds emerge from trunk vertically then arch out horizontally with great elegance. They are similar to other dicksonias,

but the undersides tend to be pale green, and rachis and stipe dark brown. Unlike the other dicksonias covered here, *D. squarrosa* occasionally produces buds at any point on the trunk: if a plant 'dies' do not throw it away as it may sprout from the base. One of the fastest growing tree ferns, when well looked after it can grow 13–15cm (5–6in) of trunk in a season. Often sold as hardy, but I know of no long-established plants outside in Britain – I overwinter it in a conservatory. It can be a little fussy: do not let it dry out or become waterlogged in winter, and avoid watering in the crown – in certain conditions this causes rots in all tree ferns, but especially here.

D. youngiae Australia – Queensland, H trunk to 2m (6ft) by 10–15cm (4–6in), fronds 1.2–2m (4–6ft) by 45cm (18in), E, wet–dry, zone 10, possibly 9. Fronds similar to other dicksonias, but rachis covered in purplish hairs. Perhaps this could be considered the Australian equivalent to *D. squarrosa*. I have never seen a trunked specimen on sale in Britain, but young sporelings on my nursery have proved remarkably hardy. Like *D. sellowiana*, it might prove much more hardy than its geographical provenance would suggest.

Doodia

A small genus of southern-hemisphere ferns, related to *Blechnum*. Sori elongate along each side of the pinna midrib.

D. media Australia, H25cm (10in), D, wet–dry, zone 8 – not reliably hardy but will succeed in a sheltered spot in warmer parts of zone 8, otherwise zone 9. Fronds narrowly lance-shaped, pinnate, red in spring. Likes acid soil.

Dryopteris

For gardeners in temperate regions, this genus offers by far the greatest number of good garden plants. Some could be considered somewhat similar, but do not dismiss this group: it contains great diversity of foliage and even some very colourful species, such as *D. erythrosora*. As a general rule, *Dryopteris* are easy to cultivate in moist, but not waterlogged, soils. They will persist for a very long time, often outliving their owners, despite neglect. Sori kidney-shaped in most species.

D. affinis (syn. *D. borreri, D. pseudomas;* **Golden male fern**) AGM Europe, including Britain, and Asia, H1–1.2m (3–4ft), W (some E), dry–wet, zone 4. Frond pinnate-pinnatifid, lance-shaped, dark green when mature. Rachis and stipe densely covered with golden-brown

scales, particularly beautiful in spring when unfurling. Although wintergreen, the fronds tend to snap and look ragged after winter snow and storms. There are several subspecies and hybrids, some of which look very similar to the more common *D. filix-mas*. To separate the two species, look at the point where the pinna joins the rachis. If there is a dark spot it is *D. affinis* or one of its hybrids; if not it is *D. filix-mas*. *D. affinis* also typically has squared tips to the pinnae segments. There are some wonderful cultivars for the garden. For the purist I have put each into its appropriate subspecies or hybrid: the hybrid is *D. × complexa* (*D. filix-mas × D. affinis*). **subsp.** *affinis* **'Crispa Gracilis'** AGM H23cm (9in), E. A beautiful little fern with erect fronds and densely overlapping pinnae, the tips of which show a hint of curling gracefully upwards. Sometimes called 'Crispa Congesta' in the trade. **subsp.** *affinis* **'Cristata'** (king of the male ferns) AGM H90cm (3ft) or more in a favoured site, W. Fronds and pinnae tips neatly crested, erect. **subsp.** *affinis* **'Cristata Angustata'** AGM H60–90cm (2–3ft), W. Pinnae and frond tips crested; elegant arching fronds are very narrow, rarely more than 6cm (2in) wide. **subsp.** *affinis* **'Pinderi'** H60–90cm (2–3ft), W. Differs from the species in having narrower fronds, and is, therefore, more elegant. Uncrested. **subsp.** *borreri* **'Polydactyla Dadds'** H90cm (3ft), D. Similar to 'Polydactyla Mapplebeck' but fronds less persistent and crests smaller; a less robust plant. **subsp.** *affinis* **'Polydactyla Mapplebeck'** AGM H1–1.2m (3–4ft), W. Similar to 'Cristata' but the fingers of the crest are longer and less regular – polydactylous. A large 'statement' fern. **subsp.** *cambrensis* **'Crispa Barnes'** H60cm (2ft), D. Similar to the species except frond crisped and far less scaly.

Above: Close-up of Dryopteris affinis 'Cristata'.

Left: Dryopteris affinis *'Cristata'.*

Dryopteris affinis *'Polydactyla Mapplebeck' in close-up.*

D. × *australis* (*D. celsa* × *D. ludoviciana*) Northeast USA, H1–1.2m (3–4ft), D, dry–wet or wet–dry, zone 5. Fronds narrow, lance-shaped, erect with a long stipe. A very handsome hybrid propagated by tissue culture. Rhizome spreads slowly, eventually forming an impressive clump.

D. bissetiana Japan, east Asia, H30–60cm (1–2ft), W, wet–dry, zone 7. Fronds triangular, bipinnate-pinnatifid, yellow-green when young, darkening with age. Rachis and stipe covered with pale scales.

D. carthusiana (**Narrow buckler fern**) Europe, H60cm (2ft), D, wet–dry, zone 3. Very similar to *D. dilatata*, but fronds narrowly lance-shaped, erect on a short creeping rhizome; scales on stipe pale brown without a darkened middle. Good in wet areas and bogs.

D. celsa (**Log fern**) North America, H60–90cm (24–36in), D, dry–wet, zone 5. Fronds pinnate-pinnatifid, erect with a long stipe. Intermediate between *D. cristata* and *D. goldiana.*

D. clintoniana North America, H60–90cm (24–36in), D, dry–wet, zone 4. Similar to *D. celsa* but fronds narrower.

Dryopteris ×
complexa *'Stablerae'*
(crisped).

D. × *complexa* **'Stablerae'** (crisped) (*D. filix-mas D.* × *affinis*) H60–75cm (24–30in), D, zone 4. Fronds lance-shaped, narrow and crisped. Also known as 'Crispa Angustata', which is a better name but apparently not correct.

D. crassirhizoma (syn. *D. buschiana*) Japan, H75cm (30in), D, dry–wet, zone 6. Fronds pinnate-pinnatifid, pale glossy green. Superficially similar to *D. affinis* and *D. wallichiana,* but the colour is distinctive in mature plants.

D. cristata (**Crested buckler fern**) Europe, very rare in Britain, and North America, H60cm (2ft), D, wet–dry, zone 3. Fronds narrow, pinnate-pinnatifid; sporing fronds erect, sterile fronds somewhat spreading.

D. cycadina AGM (see p.37) Japan, H60cm (24in), W or often E, dry–wet, zone 5. Fronds pinnate, lance-shaped, dark green with some gloss, black scales on stipe. A very striking fern, making a good robust garden plant and different from many other dryopteris.

D. dickinsii Japan, H60cm (24in), D, wet–dry, zone 6. Fronds pinnate, lance-shaped, pale green. Pinnae quite broad with lobed margins. Foliage has a pleasantly dense appearance.

D. dilatata (syn. *D. austriaca*; **Broad buckler fern**) AGM Europe, including Britain, H1–1.2m (3–4ft), W, dry–wet, zone 4. Fronds dark green, spreading, tripinnate, triangular or broadly lance-shaped, margins of pinnae often recurved. Differs from *D. carthusiana* in having dark-centred scales on the stipe. One of the most tolerant ferns – among the best for newcomers to fern growing as it copes with a wide range of conditions – and, with *D. filix-mas*, probably the commonest European fern. **'Crispa Whiteside'** AGM Paler green fronds are crisped throughout the leafy portion. **'Lepidota'** Rachis and stipe more scaly with the leafy part of the lamina narrowed, giving the frond a very airy appearance. The crested variant **'Lepidota Cristata'** AGM is most commonly found. The recurved form has margins of lamina strongly curved downwards. A pretty fern.

D. erythrosora AGM Japan, east Asia, H60cm (24in), E, dry–wet, zone 6. Fronds glossy, bipinnate, triangular, pink in spring gradually turning green with maturity. Sori usually bright red, but some plants in circulation have brown sori: these may turn out to be a different species. **'Prolifera'** AGM is more leathery and has narrower leafy parts; bulbils are sometimes formed on the frond.

D. filix-mas (**Male fern**) AGM Europe, including Britain, Asia, North America, H1–1.2m (3–4ft), D, dry–wet, zone 4. Fronds pinnate-pinnatifid, lance-shaped, more or less erect. Rhizome branches with time, producing multi-crowned clumps. One of the easiest ferns to grow in Britain. If a fern arrives unannounced in the garden, it is almost certain to be *D.filix-mas*. **'Barnesii'** Frond narrower, pinnules regularly lobed along each side, that is pinnate-pinnatifid. One of the

The red flush has disappeared in this late season Dryopteris erythrosora.

Dryopteris
filix-mas.
*Although one of the
most common hardy
ferns, it is still a
wonderful feature
here in this
Staffordshire Garden.*

tallest ferns for a well-drained border. **'Bollandiae'** H75cm–1.2m (1½–4ft). Apparently the plumose form of the species, but possibly a hybrid between *D. filix-mas* and *D. aemula*, a British native. Pinnules more lobed than in the species, and certain fronds always irregular, but not to the point where attractiveness of the fern is seriously impaired. Sori are formed but no viable spores are produced. **'Crispa Cristata'** H60cm (2ft). Fronds crested at tip and on tips of pinnae, lamina wavy (crisped). **'Crispa'** H60cm (2ft). As 'Crispa Cristata' but without the cresting. **Cristata Group** Pinnae and frond tips crested; frond not crispy. The type of cresting can vary quite markedly, so I prefer to use the group name for most plants. There are, however, some good selections in cultivation, notably **'Cristata Martindale'** in which the crests are small on the pinna and frond tips, and the pinnae near the frond tip curve up slightly towards it. **'Depauperata Padley'** H45–60cm (18–24in). Pinnules reduced, almost absent towards top of frond. Depauperate means deformed, but this fern is very pretty and well worth growing. **'Grandiceps Wills'** AGM H60–90cm (2–3ft). Pinnae tips lightly crested with a large crest at the frond tip, often exceeding the width of the frond. **'Linearis'** H60cm (24in). Frond dark green with pinnules narrowed, giving an airy appearance. In fact the frond looks fragile and delicate, although it is very robust, withstanding exposure in quite windy sites. Uncrested plants are uncommon; with maturity most develop polydactylous crests and are called **'Linearis Polydactyla'** – not 'Polydactylon' as often seen in nursery catalogues.

D. goldieana (**Goldie's fern**) North America, H1–1.2m (3–4ft), D, dry–wet, zone 4. Lamina broadly lance-shaped, almost ovate, with long stipe. Foliage somewhat yellow-green, almost gold. Very tall and rather leafy so best in a sheltered spot away from exposure to strong winds.

The flush of red fronds on Dryopteris lepidopoda *(centre) flanked by two plants of* Dryopteris neorosthornii.

D. lepidopoda Himalaya, H60cm (2ft), D, dry–wet, zone 7. Fronds lance-shaped, pinnate-pinnatifid, glossy dark green. Spring foliage a beautiful bright red.

D. marginalis North America, H60–75cm (24–30in), W, dry–wet, zone 4. Fronds bipinnate, triangular, bluish green. Sori produced on margins of pinnulets.

D. neorosthornii Himalaya, H90cm (3ft), W, dry–wet, zone 7. Like *D. wallichiana* but even better. Rachis covered with abundant black shaggy scales. Rare in cultivation.

D. pacifica East Asia, H45–60cm (18–24in), W, dry–wet, zone 8, possibly colder. Rather similar to *D. bissetiana*, but young fronds reddish, and pinna tips are acutely pointed and curve slightly to point towards the tip of the frond. Very pretty.

D. polylepis Japan, H60–90cm (2–3ft), D, dry–wet, zone 8, possibly colder. Similar to *D. crassirhizoma*, but the scales are darker and the pinnae segments are smaller and, hence, neater.

D. pseudo-filix-mas Mexico, H60–90cm (2–3ft), D, wet–dry, zone 6. Very similar to *D. filix-mas* but of interest as a fern from the tropics, albeit at high altitudes, that is hardy in cool, temperate areas.

D. pycnopteroides Japan, H60cm (2ft), E, dry–wet, zone 8. Fronds dark green glossy, pinnate, lance-shaped with strongly lacerated pinnae margins. Pinnae close together but not quite overlapping. A distinctive fern.

D. sieboldii Japan, H60cm (2ft), almost E, dry–wet, zone 6. Fronds unique in the genus – leathery, pinnate, broadly lance-shaped; pinnae margins finely serrate.

Left: Dryopteris sieboldii – *an outstanding evergreen dryopteris.*

Right: Dryopteris wallichiana *at Brodsworth Hall, Yorkshire.*

D. tokyoensis Japan, H60–90cm (2–3ft), D, dry–wet, zone 7. Fronds pinnate, narrow, lance-shaped and erect. Pinnae triangular. Unusual and very attractive.

D. uniformis Eastern Asia, H30–60cm (1–2ft), E, dry–wet, zone 6. Fronds bipinnate, slightly glossy, broadly lance-shaped. Croziers with conspicuous black scales. Rarely seen in cultivation but the cultivar '**Cristata**' is becoming less rare; it has subtle yet attractive cresting – technically more of a cristulata than a cristata.

D. wallichiana AGM Himalaya, Hawaii, Mexico, Jamaica, H60–120cm (2–4ft) rarely to 2.5m (8ft), W, dry–wet, zone 6. Fronds pinnate-pinnatifid with pinnae segments square at tip. Similar to *D. affinis*, but the rachis and stipe are very densely covered with black or brown scales. One of the most striking of all the garden ferns, this is a plant with a magnificent architectural presence: a well-grown stand would be a centre of attention in any garden.

Equisetum (Horsetails)

Although some horsetails are weeds, members of this genus make eye-catching garden plants, as long as they can be contained in a pot or tub. Certainly their popularity at horticultural shows is obvious. The main species to avoid is *E. arvense* (field horsetail): it is one of the worst weeds imaginable, its rhizomes run deep in the soil, and the take- up of herbicides on the stems is rarely enough to kill unwanted plants. It is worth considering cultivating the following species – but always in a container.

Lygodium japonicum.

E. hyemale var. *affine* (often called *E. giganteum*) North America, H to 2.5m (8ft), E, wet–dry, but not fussy, zone 7. Limey soils preferred but not essential. Stems green, up to 1cm (½in) in diameter, normally unbranched; they are easily squashed as they have a large central air cavity. When well-established and luxuriant it can become top-heavy and untidy. In spring the masses of vertical new shoots are a superb feature contrasting beautifully with virtually any other plant. *E. hyemale*, from Europe, is also worth growing, but it is smaller in all its parts, making it potentially a tidier plant.

Gymnocarpium

Although a small genus, this contains some of the prettiest garden ferns. The rhizomes creep; all can be a little invasive, but they are not likely to choke any but the most delicate plants. A mixed bed with any gymnocarpium as groundcover will be a winner with most gardeners. Spores in two rows on the underside of the pinnae; no indusium.

G. dryopteris (**Oak fern**) AGM Europe, including Britain, Asia, North America, H23–30cm (9–12in), D, wet–dry, zone 3. Fronds triangular, tripinnate on a long hairless stipe; the lamina is held at right-angles to the light, parallel to the ground, so the pretty blue-green fronds are displayed beautifully. Prefers neutral to acid soils. **'Plumosum'** AGM Has broader pinnules, allowing pinnae and pinnules to overlap. It is fertile, therefore not a true sterile plumosum.

G. robertianum (**Limestone polypody**) Europe, including Britain, Asia, North America, H15–30cm (6–12in), D, dry–wet, zone 3. Fronds similar to *G. dryopteris*, but yellow-green, slightly less leafy and with a glandular stipe. Prefers neutral to limey soils.

Gymnocarpium dryopteris *at RHS Garden Rosemoor, Devon.*

Lygodium

A genus of climbing ferns, mostly tropical. Spores are green, and therefore short-lived, borne on underturned pinna margins towards the tip of the frond. Spore-bearing pinnae are smaller than vegetative pinnae.

L. japonicum (**Japanese climbing fern**) Southeast Asia, including Japan, H1–1.5m (3–5ft), more in a heated tropical house, D, dry–wet, zone 9. Climbing fern that wraps itself around any support. Fronds tripinnate, pale green, very delicate and attractive. Pinnae spread to face light. Quite unlike any other fern described here. The hardiness of this species is the subject of much discussion. My friends in North America insist it is perfectly hardy down to zone 5 – indeed I have seen it flourishing in John Mickel's beautiful garden in New York State – but apart from a few promising reports from warm gardens, success in Britain is limited so far. As is so often the case, there is, therefore, more to hardiness than temperature; pehaps success could be achieved by keeping the roots and surrounding soil dry over winter by laying a slate over the crown?

Matteuccia

A small group of deciduous ferns with markedly dimorphic fronds: the vegetative fronds are green and pinnate-pinnatifid; the sporing fronds are pinnate and dark brown, perhaps appearing shrivelled, completely lacking any lamina. Spores green, released in winter. I am regularly asked why shuttlecock ferns start to produce dark brown fronds in late summer: it causes some concern with inexperienced owners!

M. orientalis Asia, H60–90cm (2–3ft), fertile fronds 15–23cm (6–9in), D, wet–dry, zone 7. Fronds spreading, arching away from the crown, broadly lance-shaped. Not often seen, but once established in a moist shady spot this fern does well; does not appear to spread by stolons.

M. pensylvanica is a very closely related American species that produces less tidy and rather more spreading crowns, making the sporing fronds appear longer.

M. struthiopteris (**Shuttlecock fern, ostrich fern**) AGM Europe, not Britain, North America, H1–1.5m (3–5ft), fertile fronds 30–45cm (12–18in), D, wet, zone 3. Fronds narrowly lance-shaped, almost vertical, in a regular shuttlecock form, especially when unfurling. They are produced on an erect rhizome which can become almost trunk-like, up to 15cm (6in) high, but stolons are also produced just under the soil surface and lead to the rapid formation of colonies in favourably moist conditions. There is no warning where a new plant might appear, all of a sudden a new crown shows up perhaps 30cm (12in) away from the parent. If new crowns appear in inconvenient sites, they can be lifted easily and the underground stolons cut.

Onoclea

Only one species, but one of the best garden ferns for damp or wet conditions. As in *Matteuccia*, the fronds are strongly dimorphic.

O. sensibilis AGM North America, H60cm (24in), D, wet, zone 2. Vegetative fronds pinnate or pinnatifid with wavy pinna margins, green on a long stipe; sporing fronds brown, lamina reduced to dark-

Right: Onoclea sensibilis.

Left: Matteuccia pensylvanica *at Nacogdoches, Texas, USA.*

brown globular structures near the tip. Young vegetative fronds are usually green, but are bright red in some clones in cultivation.

Onychium (Carrot ferns)

A small group of very distinctive species. Sori marginal, linear.

O. japonicum East Asia, Japan, H30–45cm (12–18in), D, dry–wet, zone 8. Fronds triangular, tripinnate on a long stipe, resembling carrot leaves. Needs a sheltered site to thrive.

Onychium japonicum *in a Staffordshire garden.*

Oreopteris

A small genus, related to *Thelypteris*. Sori circular, lacking indusium, arranged in a row along each side of the pinnae segments, midway between the central vein and the margin.

O. limbosperma (syn. *Thelypteris limbosperma*; Lemon-scented fern) Europe, including Britain, D, wet–dry, zone 4. Rarely cultivated. Fronds elliptic, pinnate-pinnatifid, pale green with tiny pinnae retracing to the base of the frond, hence virtually no stipe. Crushed fronds smell pleasantly of lemon.

Osmunda

A smallish genus of often very large ferns that are ideal for wet places. Virtually all species are excellent garden plants. All show some dimorphism: the sporing fronds are markedly different from standard vegetative fronds. Spore-bearing parts are reduced to masses of sporangia, and there is no lamina. Spores are green and short-lived, so best sown within a few days of harvest, although will survive longer if kept in a fridge.

Osmunda cinnamomea

O. cinnamomea AGM North America, H60cm–1.2m (2–4ft), D, wet–dry, zone 2. Fronds dimorphic: vegetative fronds pinnate-pinnatifid, pale green, lance-shaped, held at about 30 degrees from the vertical in a shuttlecock effect around the erect sporing fronds, which are pinnate, usually 20 per cent taller than vegetative fronds; they have no lamina, the pinnae are erect and parallel to the main rachis. The top half of the sporing frond is densely covered with sporangia, which turn cinnamon-brown at maturity. When sporing, the whole plant is somewhat reminiscent of an *Astilbe*. A fascinating fern and a great beauty, sadly not as quick to reach maturity as most other species.

O. claytoniana (**Interrupted fern**) AGM North America, H60–90cm (2–3ft), D, wet–dry, zone 2. Fronds dimorphic: vegetative fronds are like *O. cinnamomea*, but the pinnae segments are crenately margined; the sporing fronds are held erect, but only the middle section is soriferous. Here the leafy pinnae are completely replaced by black spore masses. A striking plant, perhaps slightly less attractive than the closely related *O. cinnamomea* but, nevertheless, very well worth growing in a wettish border. Looks particularly good in groups of three to five plants.

O. regalis (**Royal fern, flowering fern**) AGM Europe, including Britain, Asia, H1.2–2m (4–6ft), D, wet, zone 3. Fronds broadly lance-shaped, bipinnate, pinnules broad-oblong, usually with smooth margins. More or less erect mid-season fronds bear spores at the tips, the pinnules completely replaced by spore masses. The brown tips bear a superficial resemblance to flowers, hence the common name. In drought situations it is always the sporing fronds that die back first. In autumn the dying foliage is butter-yellow for a few days, turning to a distinctive shade of brown by midwinter. This is the very best fern for waterside planting, where it can easily exceed 2m (6ft). A very long-lived fern, it eventually produces a huge rootstock, almost a small fibrous trunk and much sought after by orchid growers. '**Cristata**' AGM H1–1.2m (3–4ft). More compact with pinnae, pinnules and frond tip all crested, or at least forked. To be technically accurate it is a percristatum, but I think we can safely leave it as cristata. Beware – plants offered as 'Cristata' are often plain. '**Purpurascens**' Possibly from the Atlantic Islands, H1–1.2m (3–4ft). Pinnae more widely spaced and all foliage is purple when young; midribs, rachis and stipe

This specimen of Osmunda regalis at Muncaster Castle, Cumbria, is over 2.2m (7ft) tall.

retain the purple colour all season. Immature plants are often only weakly coloured, while some never colour up at all. **'Undulatifolia'** (syn. **'Crispa'**, **'Undulata'**) H1–1.2m (3–4ft). This has a wavy lamina and the stipe, rachis and midribs are all straight. A pretty fern with an awful name! I prefer **'Undulata'** but am told **'Undulatifolia'** has precedence.

Paesia

A single species with connections to bracken.

P. scaberula (**Ring fern**) New Zealand, H30–60cm (1–2ft), D, dry–wet but not critical, zone 7. Needs acid soil. Fronds tripinnate, lance-shaped, pale green, borne on a short creeping rhizome. Pinnae are produced alternately up the rachis, causing it to zig-zag slightly.

Phegopteris

Left: Paesia scaberula.

Right: Phegopteris connectilis *at Branklyn, Perth, Scotland.*

A small genus once placed in *Thelypteris*. Sori round with no indusium, produced in rows midway between the midrib of the pinnae segments and their margin.

P. connectilis (syn. *Thelypteris phegopteris*; **Beech fern**) Europe, including Britain, Asia, North America, H15–40cm (6–16in), D, wet–dry, zone 2. Best in acid soil in moist shade. Fronds pinnate-pinnatifid, appearing ovate because the basal pair of pinna points forward from the rachis. Stipe long. Rhizome creeping.

P. decursive-pinnata (syn. *Thelypteris decursive-pinnata*; **Japanese beech fern**) Central and eastern Asia, H45cm (18in), D, wet–dry, zone 5. Fronds narrowly lance-shaped, almost elliptic, pinnate-pinnatifid. Rhizome more or less erect, sometimes short-creeping. Nothing like *P. connectilis.*

P. hexagonoptera (syn. *Thelypteris hexagonoptera;* **Broad beech fern**)
North America, H30–45cm (12–18in), D, wet–dry, zone 5. Similar to
P. connectilis, but the frond is broader and bipinnatifid (the basal pinnae
are attached to the next pair of pinnae by a wing of lamina).

Polypodium

A large genus, formerly much larger but many groups have been split
off into separate genera. Fronds usually leathery; sori round, without an
indusium, produced in single rows midway between the midrib of the
pinnae and their margin. All polypodiums here need a well-drained and
well-ventilated site. In very humid conditions leaf blotching can occur.

P. australe (syn. *P. cambricum*; **Southern polypody**) South and west
Europe, including Britain, Asia, North Africa, H7–60cm (3–24in), W,
dry–wet, zone 6. In the face of much botanical opinion to the
contrary, I am persisting with the species name *P. australe* instead of the
more politically correct *P. cambricum*. For over 200 years Cambricum
has been synonymous with the Cambricum Group of cultivars; to
change now causes unneeded confusion, especially as it will very likely
change back again in the future. Fronds pinnatifid, ovate, almost
deltate, longest pair of pinnae usually the
second from the base, pinnae rapidly
reduce in size towards the tip of the frond.
Pinna margins finely serrate. Rhizomes
covered in pale brown scales creep on or
near the surface. Fronds are produced in
late summer, remain fresh and green
throughout winter, dying back in spring;
they are invisible in late spring and early
summer. A wonderful plant that, together
with its cultivars, should be more widely
grown – I can think of no other
herbaceous plant giving such beautiful
fresh foliage throughout winter. In the
wild it almost always grows on limestone
rock or well-drained lime-rich ground. In
Britain it has a particular affinity with

Polypodium
australe
*'Cambricum' base
form.*

castle walls. **Cambricum Group** A group of the most beautiful
cultivars, all sterile (so propagation is by sectioning the rhizome) and
with deeply lacerated pinnae. They are difficult to distinguish from
one another unless well grown. Base form **'Cambricum'** AGM is the
one most usually seen. It has papery and broadly ovate fronds with finely

lacerated and slightly twisted pinnae. **'Barrowii'** is rare. It has pinnae with broad serrations; lamina twisted, leathery, slightly glossy, broadly ovate. **'Prestonii'** also rare, fronds with broad serrations, lamina twisted, leathery, slightly glossy, lance-shaped. **'Whilharris'** AGM quite common, often misidentified as 'Barrowii', fronds with broad serrations, lamina twisted, leathery, slightly glossy, frond outline is lance-shaped, but almost parallel-sided, separating it from 'Prestonii'. The best of the cambricum section is **'Richard Kayse'** (true Welsh polypody; p.6–7), which is most similar to the base form, but the lamina on each pinna is not twisted and the serrations are more regular. It is a very rare form first discovered in 1668, making all material of this cultivar over one-third of a millennium old – since all material is produced vegetatively from the original stock. **'Cristatum'** Frond and pinnae tips have twisted crests. Rare. The terminal crest is often slightly depauperate and narrower than the frond lamina. **Grandiceps Group** As 'Cristatum', but all crests are heavier, and the terminal crest is not depauperate and is wider than the frond lamina.

Polypodium australe 'Semilacerum Falcatum O'Kelly'.

There are three named forms, all rare; the one most often seen is **'Grandiceps Fox'** AGM. **'Hornet'** Fronds irregularly oblong, all tips terminate in a distinct bristle. **'Macrostachyon'** Like the species except that the tip of the frond is extended into a narrow elongated tip. **'Omnilacerum Superbum'** (syn. 'Omnilacerum Oxford') A tall form, H to 75cm (30in), all pinnae, except a few approaching the frond tip, are finely lacerated (bipinnatifid), as in 'Cambricum'; spores are freely produced. **Pulcherrimum Group** Fronds regularly bipinnatifid or even tripinnatifid if well grown. There are several very similar cultivars in this group; all are fertile, albeit often sparsely. Pinnae more or less flat. **'Pulchritudine'** A selected form of pulcherimum with pinnae and segments slightly crisped. **Semilacerum Group** As the species, but the lower half of the pinnae are usually lacerated. The lacerations are usually blunt, unlike 'Omnilacerum Superbum'. Fronds pale green. There are some good named forms: **'Falcatum O'Kelly'**, with sickle-shaped pinnae, bipinnatifid in the mid-part of the frond; **'Robustum'** has dark green, leathery fronds.

P. glycyrrhiza (**Liquorice fern**) Northwest USA, H45–60cm (18–24in), E, dry–wet, zone 6. Fronds dark green, papery, pinnatifid, narrowly lance-shaped, almost oblong. Pinna margins slightly serrate. Rhizome tastes of licorice. There are some very good cultivars: **'Longicaudatum'** AGM As species except fronds have a long, drawn-out tip (see p.10). **'Malahatense'** Sterile along the lines of 'Cambricum' in *P. australe*. Very pretty but not such a strong grower. A very similar form which is fertile, with pinnae that are not so finely serrated, seems to lack a proper name: I call it **'Malahatense – fertile form'**.

P. interjectum (**Intermediate polypody**) Europe, including Britain, H45cm (18in), E, dry–wet, zone 5. Likes neutral to limey soils and rocks. Frond pinnatifid, lance-shaped, leathery; longest pair of pinnae is usually about the sixth from the base of the frond. Fully fertile; indusium full of yellow sporangia when mature. Fronds produced in midsummer.

P. × *mantoniae* (*P. vulgare* × *P. interjectum*) Europe, including Britain, H45cm (18in), E, dry–wet, zone 5. Very similar to *P. interjectum*, but sporangia are mainly brown and abortive, sparingly fertile or not fertile. *P. interjectum* sometimes produces abortive sporangia, so these two taxa are extremely difficult to separate without a full chromosome count. **'Bifido-grandiceps'** Probably arose in cultivation as a hybrid between *P. interjectum* and *P. vulgare* 'Bifido-cristatum'. Pinnae and frond tips flat-crested, terminal crest broader than the frond. **'Cornubiense'** AGM (see p.24) Probably arose

Polypodium vulgare *'Elegantissimum' in Staffordshire.*

in cultivation as a hybrid between *P. interjectum* and *P. vulgare* 'Elegantissimum'. Justifiably a widely grown cultivar with two types of frond: one as normal *P.* × *mantoniae*, the other fully bipinnatifid; occasionally some fronds are partly one type, partly the other. Sterile.

P. vulgare (**Common polypody**) Europe, including Britain, Asia, H38cm (15in), E, dry–wet, zone 3. Likes neutral to acid soils, often epiphytic on trees in high rainfall areas. Fronds papery and pinnatifid, narrow – uniform width throughout most of their length. Indusium orange-brown when ripe. Fully fertile. **'Bifido-cristatum'** Pinnae and frond tips flat-crested, terminal crest broader than frond. **'Cornubiense Grandiceps'** A crested form of 'Elegantissimum' with two or three types of frond, none quadripinnatifid. **'Elegantissimum'** (syn. **'Cornubiense'**, **'Whytei'**) An extraordinary cultivar that produces three types of fronds: one like the species, another bipinnatifid, and the third tri- or quadripinnatifid. A rather uncommon cultivar that does not grow strongly with me in slightly alkaline soil, but flourishes on acid soil in Joyce Hayward's Staffordshire garden. **'Jean Taylor'** (syn. **'Congestum Cristatum'**) A dwarf crested form of 'Elegantissimum' with some quadripinnatifid fronds. A gem, but rarely in character. **'Ramosum Hillman'** Like the species, except that the frond branches, usually into three parts, near its base. Each part then forks again at its tip. **'Trichomanoides Backhouse'** Like 'Elegantissimum' but only two types of frond: normal and quadripinnatifid, and it is altogether more finely cut than 'Elegantissimum'.

Polystichum

The rare and beautiful Polypodium australe *'Cambricum Prestonii'.*

A large genus, together with *Dryopteris* producing the largest number of first-class ferns for temperate gardens. *Polystichum* species occur in most parts of the world, from high mountains to tropical forests, with the largest concentration in eastern Asia from the Himalaya to Japan. In recent years new species have been introduced into cultivation from this region; most are still rare and often unnamed, but be prepared to encounter unfamiliar ones in specialist nurseries. Virtually

73

all are evergreen, often with a hard, bristly texture. Sporangia are produced in circular indusia in rows along each side of the ultimate frond segment, midway between the segment margin and its midrib. All polystichums like well-drained sites – a moist shady bank should see them luxuriate. In certain conditions they are susceptible to a very unpleasant disease, *Taphrina wettsteiniana* (see p.28).

P. acrostichoides (**Christmas fern**) Eastern North America, H60cm (2ft) rarely 90cm (3ft), E, dry–wet, zone 3. Fronds dark green, pinnate, narrow. Pinna tips often blunt. Pinnae dimorphic: pinnae bearing spores are reduced in size and restricted to the tips of the frond. The common name refers to the evergreen nature of the fronds.

P. aculeatum (**Hard shield fern**) AGM Europe, including Britain, H75–90cm (30–36in), E, dry–wet, zone 4. Fronds bipinnate, lance-shaped, darkish glossy green; pinnules unstalked. In the wild sometimes difficult to separate from *P. setiferum* with which it hybridizes. The hybrid can only be reliably identified by inspection for abortive spores or by chromosome counts. *P. aculeatum* can be distinguished from *P. setiferum* by the acute angle at the base of the pinnule where it is attached to the pinna midrib: in *P. setiferum* this angle is 90 degrees or more; the pinnules are also usually stalked. In *P. aculeatum* the frond stipe is very short, usually about 2.5cm (1in), while in *P. setiferum* it is much longer. A common fern that produces no cultivars of great merit but makes a beautiful garden plant. Probably my favourite British native species.

P. braunii Central Europe, North America, eastern Asia, H60–90cm (24–36in), E, dry–wet, zone 4. Very similar to *P. setiferum,* from which it differs mainly in having slightly shiny pale green fronds covered with hairs. Included here because many plants in horticulture are doubtfully this species.

P. imbricans Western North America, H30–60cm (1–2ft), E, dry–wet, zone 6. Fronds pinnate, congested, dark green. Very similar to *P. munitum*, from which it has only recently been separated. *P. imbricans* has more congested fronds.

P. luctuosum South Africa, eastern Asia, H30–60cm (1–2ft), E, dry–wet, zone 8. Fronds bipinnate, leathery, dull dark green. Similar to *P. tsus-simense* but less finely cut and, therefore, generally more leafy.

P. munitum (**Western sword fern**) AGM North-west America, H90cm (36in), E, dry–wet, zone 6. Fronds narrowly lance-shaped, pinnate, dark green, glossy. Superficially similar to *P. acrostichoides* but pinnae not dimorphic and pinna tips more pointed. Well grown fronds can reach 1.2–1.5m (4–5ft) long, even in full sun if in moist soil, making this one of the largest evergreen ferns hardy in Britain (only beaten by *Blechnum chilense*).

Left: Polystichum neolobatum.

Right: The attractive croziers of Polystichum neolobatum.

P. neolobatum Japan, eastern Asia, H45cm (18in), E, dry–wet, zone 7. Fronds lance-shaped, glossy dark green, bipinnate, very stiff and prickly to the touch. A beautiful fern, particularly in crozier, i.e. when the fronds are unfurling.

P. nepalense Himalaya, H30–45cm (12–18in), E, dry–wet, zone 7. Fronds dark green, pinnate, oblong. No 'thumb' on the acroscopic side of the pinnae. A beautiful fern, still rare. Very distinctive.

P. polyblepharum AGM (see p.76) Japan, H45–60cm (18–24in), E, dry–wet, zone 6. Fronds bipinnate, lance-shaped to triangular, less tough to the touch than *P. neolobatum*, glossy green covered with golden bristles that are particularly noticeable on the croziers.

P. proliferum (**Mother shield fern**) Australia, H45–90cm (18–36in), E, dry–wet, zone 8. Fronds lance-shaped, bipinnate, dark green. Produces one or two buds on the rachis near the tip of fronds on mature plants. Can grow large rootstocks – almost trunks.

Polystichum polyblepharum *in a Cumberland garden.*

P. rigens Japan, H38cm (15in), E, dry–wet, zone 6. Fronds pale to mid-green, lance-shaped – triangular on young plants – bipinnate. All tips very stiff and acutely pointed. In summer the fronds smell of skunk; perhaps I am odd but I don't find it unpleasant!

P. setiferum (**Soft shield fern**) AGM Europe, including Britain, H75–90cm (30–36in), E, dry–wet, zone 5. Fronds bi- to tripinnate, lance-shaped, mid-green. General frond texture soft for a polystichum. Angle at base of pinnule where it is attached to the pinna midrib is 90 degrees or more (see *P. aculeatum*). *P. setiferum* has been a prolific producer of fine cultivars; the ones most commonly encountered commercially are described here. '**Acutilobum**' This cultivar breaks all the rules: it has an angle of less than 90 degrees at the base of its pinnules where they attach the pinna midrib, it also has a very short stipe. The pinnules are undivided but do have a small 'thumb' near their base. It is very easily confused with *P. aculeatum*, from which it can be distinguished in that it is more spiky on the tips of the pinnules and its 'thumb'. Rare in cultivation; does not produce bulbils. A lot of divisilobums have in the past been classed as acutilobum in error; divisilobums frequently produce bulbils. '**Congestum**' Like the species, but the rachis and pinnae midribs are short, causing the pinnae and pinnules to overlap. Stipe and rachis

Bottom left: Polystichum setiferum 'Congestum'.

Bottom right: Polystichum setiferum 'Cristato-pinnulum'.

Polystichum setiferum 'Divisilobum' at Barnard Green House, Great Malvern, Worcestershire.

stout and rather brittle. Forms with crested tips ('Congestum Cristatum') or with very large terminal crests ('Congestum Grandiceps') can occur in sowings. **'Cristato-pinnulum'** Fronds bipinnate with flabellate (fan-shaped) pinnules, frond often, but not always, proliferous. **'Dahlem'** Fronds narrowly triangular, bipinnate, more leafy than the species, approaching divisilobum. Fronds held more erect than most *P. setiferum* cultivars. Plants in cultivation are usually spore-grown and can differ one to another. **'Divisilobum'** Hard-textured fronds, lance-shaped or narrowly triangular, up

Above: Polystichum setiferum 'Divisilobum Trilobum'.

to tripinnate, rarely quadripinnate; final segments very narrow, elongated and pointed. Often confused with 'Multilobum', which has wider final segments and is more leafy and softer than 'Divisilobum'. Divisilobum is a section where dozens, perhaps a hundred, different clones have been named in the past. Today it is a good idea to follow the group-naming concept and refer to plants of unknown or spore provenance as Divisilobum Group. **'Gracillimum'** Progeny of 'Plumosum Bevis' with fronds bipinnate, lax, spreading; small tassles, not crests, appear on pinna tips. Until recently a very rare, sterile cultivar; now a clone called **'Green Lace'** has been tissue cultured in Holland. Very beautiful. **'Herrenhausen'** A clone of 'Divisilobum', selected for spore propagation and now quite common. Fronds spreading, triangular to lance-shaped, tripinnate. **'Iveryanum'** (syn. **'Divisilobum Iveryanum'**) AGM A crested form of divisilobum, usually proliferous. A related but different form called **'Divisilobum Trilobum'** (syn. **'Caput Trifidum'**) has very wide terminal crests. **'Multilobum'** Like 'Divisilobum', but ultimate segments (pinnulets) resemble small versions of the pinnae, unlike divisilobum in which the pinnulets are narrow and acutely pointed. Often bulbiferous. **'Plumoso-divisilobum'** A rare group of cultivars. Fronds lance-shaped, approaching deltate, often quadripinnate near frond base, soft-

Polystichum setiferum *'Plumoso-divisilobum Bland'* in *early summer.*

textured, ultimate segments narrow and acutely pointed. **'Plumoso-divisilobum Deltoideum'** is a superb clone with strongly triangular fronds. **'Plumoso-divisilobum Bland'** is another fine form, first found wild in Northern Ireland. **'Plumoso-multilobum'** (syn. **'Plumoso-densum'**, **'Divisilobum Densum'**) AGM A common type of cultivar, very beautiful but particularly susceptible to *Taphrina wettsteiniana* (see p.28). Fronds quadripinnate, almost deltate, soft-textured, ultimate segments broad and like a tiny version of the pinnule of the species. Often bulbiferous. Perhaps the most remarkable example of cultivar development in any species of fern. **Plumosum Group** Another group of very choice cultivars. Typically, the fronds are feathery and sterile;

'Plumosum Bevis' does not really fit this description, but for the time being I will treat it here. 'Plumosum Bevis' (syn. 'Pulcherrimum Bevis') AGM Fronds lance-shaped, bipinnate, dark green, glossy. Tip of frond and tips of pinnae appear plaited, as the segments are falcate and curve towards the tip of the frond or pinna. Usually sterile, but a patient hand-lens search of the underside of fronds of a mature plant might reveal a sorus, or more likely a few clumps of sporangia. If found these should be treasured as they can produce wonderful cultivars: 'Gracillimum' (see above); 'Plumosum Drueryi', completely sterile and very rare, like 'Plumosum Bevis' except that the fronds tend to be tripinnate; 'Plumosum Green', fronds lance-shaped to triangular, tri- or quadripinnate, pale green – I suspect this plant may be a sterile hybrid between 'Plumosum Bevis' and a 'Divisilobum'. Extremely rare and, frustratingly, extremely beautiful. 'Plumosum Moly' H90cm (36in). Fronds lance-shaped, tripinnatifid, pinnules broad and leafy, overlapping, sterile. Very rare. **Ramo-pinnum Group** Fronds lance-shaped, pinnae branched, not crested at tip, particularly near middle of frond. Frond tip usually unbranched. 'Wakleyanum' Fronds narrow, almost oblong. Pinnae cruciate (cross-shaped), that is, they branch at the point of contact with the rachis; they are also reduced in length. The original clone of this cultivar is probably extinct, but cruciate plants of *P. setiferum* are seen occasionally.

Polystichum setiferum *'Plumosum Bevis'*.

P. tsus-simense AGM Korea, east Asia. H30cm (1ft), E, dry–wet, zone 7. Fronds lance-shaped, bi- to tripinnate. All tips acutely pointed, dull green.

P. vestitum New Zealand, H30–90cm (1-3ft), E, dry–wet, zone 8. Fronds lance-shaped, bipinnate, dark glossy green above, pale below. Rachis and stipe densely covered with brown scales. Very beautiful.

Selaginella

A very large genus of moss-like plants mostly from the tropics. A few are hardy or half-hardy. Only one has proved a good consistent garden plant.

S. kraussiana AGM Africa, H2.5–5cm (1–2in), E, wet–dry but not fussy, zone 6. Short, creeping stems branch frequently to form a dense green carpet. In a cool conservatory, it will spread across stone floors. Shopping around in garden centres may reveal coloured forms, such as **'Aurea'** (golden) and **'Variegata'** AGM (white variegated).

Thelypteris

Formerly a large genus, now much reduced as groups of species have been renamed. They are very 'ferny' ferns. Sori have no indusium and are produced in single rows each side of the pinnule midrib halfway to the pinnule margin.

T. kunthii (syn. *T. normalis*) South-east USA, H60cm (2ft), D, wet–dry, zone 9. Fronds pinnate-pinnatifid, broadly lance-shaped to oblong on a long stipe, pale yellow green. Sporing and vegetative fronds similar.

T. palustris Europe, North America. H vegetative fronds 60cm (24in), sporing fronds 90cm (3ft) in ideal conditions, D, wet, zone 4. Fronds pinnate-pinnatifid, lance-shaped to oblong on a long slender stipe, bluish green, erect on a creeping rhizome. All parts of sporing fronds are narrower than vegetative fronds, with the pinnule margin rolled under. The North American form is slightly hairy and treated as var. *pubescens*.

Todea

A small genus from the *Osmunda* family.

T. barbara Australasia, South Africa, H1.2m (4ft), D, wet, zone 8. A magnificent fern, up to 2m (6ft) tall in nature. Fronds lance-shaped, bipinnate, from a massive rootstock. Some plants that have been grown under glass for a hundred years or more, for example at Ascog fernery on the Isle of Bute, Scotland, have produced massive trunks 1m (3ft) or more high and 70cm–1m (2–3ft) in diameter. Spores are green, carried only on basal half of pinna on well-established plants.

Woodsia

A genus of 30 or so species of small alpine fern. Spores are produced in a cup-shaped indusium; the cup may be entire, but it is more often deeply cut. Two native British species, *W. ilvensis* and *W. alpina*, are too rare to consider here.

W. obtusa North America, H15–30cm (6–12in), D, dry–wet, zone 3. Fronds lance-shaped, bipinnate, light green; pinnules rounded at tip. Rachis scaly. One of the first species to green up in spring.

W. polystichoides AGM Eastern Asia, H5–15cm (2–6in), D, dry–wet, zone 5. Fronds oblong, narrow, pinnate, dark green, superficially similar to a small polystichum. A very pretty fern but rarely available recently. One of the very best ferns for rock work.

Woodwardia (Chain ferns)

Large ferns with oblong sori arranged in rows on the underside of the frond, close to the pinnule midrib – with some imagination they seem to form a chain-like pattern.

W. fimbriata (**Giant chain fern**) Western North America, H60cm–2m (2–6ft), E, wet–dry, zone 8. Frond lance-shaped, pinnate-pinnatifid, pinnule margins finely serrate. All fronds green all season. Fronds more or less erect, not bulbiferous. A rare case of a fern for wet conditions that is more or less evergreen.

W. radicans (**European chain fern**) AGM Southwest Europe, including Atlantic Islands, H0.3–2.2m (1–7ft), E, wet–dry, zone 9. Fronds similar to *W. fimbriata,* except that they arch and root at the tip where they produce one or two bulbils. Young fronds yellowish, sometimes with a transient hint of red. Not hardy with me in Central England.

W. unigemmata Himalayas to Taiwan, H30cm–2.2m (1–7ft), E, wet–dry, zone 8. Similar to *W. radicans,* except that it is hardier and the new fronds are red for a week or two as they unfurl. One of the very best garden ferns; I plant the crown under a stone slab for protection from excess winter damp and cold.

FURTHER INFORMATION

GARDENS TO VISIT

In almost any city in the world there is a botanic garden: too many to list here. Most have a good collection of ferns, although there is a bias towards more tropical species.

Australia

Rippon Lea, Elsternwick, Melbourne. A wonderful Victorian fernery, recently restored by the Fern Society of Victoria.

Britain

In addition to the gardens listed, many Cornish gardens, such as **Trebah, Trengwainton, Carwinion, Penjerrick, Trewidden, Caerhays Castle** and **Heligan**, are worth a visit to see luxuriant tree ferns.

Ascog Fernery, Ascog, Isle of Bute. Wonderful, very well stocked Victorian glasshouse fernery.

Brodsworth Hall (English Heritage), Doncaster, Yorkshire. A Victorian fernery recently planted with the Eric Baker fern collection together with a very good selection of tree ferns.

Barnard Green House, Great Malvern, Worcestershire. Many hardy ferns featured in large garden.

Chelsea Physic Garden, 66 Hospital Road, London SW3. The Victorian base of the great fern man Thomas Moore. Still a good collection under glass and outside.

Crystal Palace Park, London, SE19. This is potentially the largest fern garden in the world, and when it is established it should be stunning.

Inside the Victorian fernery at Ascog Hall on the Isle of Bute, Scotland.

Dyffryn Park, near Cardiff, Wales. Large, recently planted fernery.

Glasgow Botanic Garden, 730 Great Western Road, Glasgow G12 0UE. This must be mentioned for the fantastic Kibble Palace, which is currently under restoration but contains the National Collection of *Dicksonia*.

Greencombe Gardens Trust, Porlock, Somerset TA24 8NU. National Collection of *Polystichum*. One of my favourite gardens.

RHS Garden Harlow Carr, Crag Lane, Harrogate, Yorkshire HG3 1QB. National Collections of *Dryopteris* and *Polypodium*; moves afoot to increase the collections.

Inverewe (National Trust for Scotland), Poolewe, Ross-shire IV22 2LG. Woodland ferns including tree ferns.

Ivycroft Plants, Ivington Green, Leominster, Herefordshire HR6 0JN. The garden has a select collection of well-grown ferns, and there are some for sale.

Knightshayes Court (National Trust), Tiverton, Devon EX16 7RG. A good selection of woodland ferns in garden.

Holehird (Lakeland Horticultural Society), Ullswater Road, Windermere, Cumbria LA23 1NP. National Collection of *Polystichum*.

RHS Garden Rosemoor, Great Torrington, Devon EX38 8PH. Ferns scattered through the garden but particularly in a rock cutting.

Royal Botanic Gardens, Kew, Richmond, Surrey TW9 3AB. One of the largest collections, mainly in greenhouses; sadly the filmy fern house has now gone.

Savill Garden (Crown Estates), Englefield Green, Egham,

Surrey TW20 0UU. Huge collection in woodland. General National Collection of ferns.

Sizergh Castle (National Trust), Kendal, Cumbria LA8 8AE. National Collections of *Asplenium*, *Dryopteris*, *Osmunda* and *Cystopteris* in a rock-garden setting.

Tatton Park, Knutsford, Cheshire WA16 6QN. Magnificent Victorian tree fern house.

RHS Garden Wisley, Woking, Surrey GU23 6QB. Large collection scattered throughout the gardens.

France

Conservatoire Botanique Nationale de Brest, 52 Allée du Bot, 29200 Brest.

Ireland

As in England, there many gardens in the southwest with wonderful stands of tree ferns; these include **Fota, Cork; Glanleam, Kerry; Kells House, Kerry; Dereen, Kerry.**

Netherlands

Hortus Botannicus Leiden, Rapenburg 73, Leiden. Huge outdoor fernery and large glasshouse collection.

New Zealand

Pukekura Park, New Plymouth. A wonderful, old, part – subterranean fernery, with ferns in park.

North America

Many gardens have some ferns (see Rickard, 2000 for fuller list). The best contact in the USA is the Hardy Fern Foundation, PO Box 166, Medina, Washington 98039-0166. **New York Botanic Garden**, Bronx, New York 10458. Under glass and outside, includes the F. Gordon Foster collection.

South Africa

Kirstenbosch Botanic Gardens, Kirstenbosch, near Cape Town. Ferns in the garden and above, wild, on Table Mountain.

WHERE TO BUY FERNS
Australia

Below are three nurseries I have visited in Victoria; there are others in New South Wales and elsewhere that I have not seen.

Austral Ferns, 25 Cozens Road, Lara, Victoria 3212.
Fernworld, 572 Heatherton Road, Springvale South, Melbourne, Victoria 3172.
Mr Fern, 260 Amiets Road, Wyelangta, Victoria 3249.

Britain

Fibrex Nurseries, Honeybourne Road, Pebworth, Stratford-on-Avon, Warwickshire CV37 8XT, Tel: 01789 720788, Fax: 01789 721162, **www.fibrex.co.uk**
Long Acre Nursery, Dunkirk, South Lane, Southbourne, Emsworth, Hampshire PO10 8PR, Tel: 01243 375388.
Reginald Kaye, Waithman Nurseries, Lindeth Road, Silverdale, Carnforth, Lancashire LA5 0TY, Tel: 01524 701252.
Rickard's Hardy Ferns Ltd., Carreg y Fedwen, Sling, Tregarth, Nr Bangor, Caernarvonshire, North Wales, LL57 4RP, Tel/Fax: 01248 602944 (send five first class stamps for catalogue).
The Fern Nursery, Grimsby Road, Binbrook, Lincolnshire LN3 6DH (send SAE for list), Tel: 01472 398092; **www.fernnursery.co.uk**

Chile

Vivero Rio Tijeral, Ruta 215, Osorno, Tel: (00 56) (64) 230934, **www.viveronline.cl** Good selection of native Chilean species.

Netherlands

D J Tas & Zonen, Uiterweg 266-272, 1431 AV Aalsmeer.

USA

Fancy Fronds, PO Box 1090, Gold Bar, WA 98215 (send $2 for catalogue), Tel: (00 1) (360) 793 1472, Fax: (00 1) (360) 793 4243, **www.fancyfronds.com**
Foliage Gardens, 2003, 128th Avenue SE, Bellevue, WA 98005 (send $2 for catalogue), Tel: (425) 747 2998, **www.foliagegardens.com**

FERN SOCIETIES

Australia

Fern Society of Australia, PO Box 45, Heidelberg, Victoria 3081.

Britain

British Pteridological Society, Mr M. Porter, 5 West Avenue, Wigton, Cumbria CA7 9LG. The oldest fern society in the world, with around 800 members.

Netherlands

Nederlandse Varenvereniging, Dhr. R.P. Huibers, Dwarspad, 15, 1721 BP Broek op Langedijk.

New Zealand

Nelson Fern Society Inc. of New Zealand, Mrs J Bonnington, 9 Bay View Road, Atawhai, Nelson.

North America

American Fern Society, Dr D B Lellinger, 326 West Street NW, Vienna, VA 22180-4151.

Hardy Fern Foundation, PO Box 166, Medina, WA 98039-0166.

Los Angeles International Fern Society, PO Box 90943, Pasadena, CA 91109-0943.

San Diego Fern Society, Robin Halley, 1418 Park Row, La Jolla, CA 92037.

Switzerland

Schweizerische Verinigung der Farnfreunde, Dr M. Zink, Institut fur systematische Botanik der Universitat, Zollikerstrasse 107, CH 8008 Zurich.

NATIONAL COLLECTIONS OF FERNS

Britain

General ferns: Savill and Valley Gardens, Windsor Great Park, Windsor, Berkshire SL4 2HT. Tel: 01753 860222.

British Ferns: Alastair Wardlaw, 92 Drymen Road, Bearsden, Glasgow G61 2SY. Tel: 0141 942 2461.

Asplenium: Sizergh Castle (National Trust), Kendal, Cumbria LA8 8AE. Tel: 015395 60496.

Asplenium: Jack Bouckley, 209 Woodfield Road, Harrogate, North Yorkshire HG1 4JE. Tel: 01423 566948.

Athyrium: Nick Schroder, 2 The Dell, Haywards Heath, Sussex RH16 1JG. Tel: 01444 415271.

Cystopteris: Sizergh Castle (as Asplenium, above).

Dicksoniaceae: Glasgow Botanic Garden, Glasgow G12 0UE. Tel: 0141 334 2422

Dryopteris: RHS Garden Harlow Carr, Crag Lane, Harrogate, Yorkshire HG3 1QB. Tel: 01423 565418.

Dryopteris: Sizergh Castle (as Asplenium, above).

Equisetum; Anthony Pigott, Kersey's Farm, Mendlesham, Stowmarket, Suffolk IP14 5RB. Tel: 01449 766104.

Osmunda; A. R. Busby, 16 Kirby Corner Road, Canley, Coventry, West Midlands CV4 8GD. Tel: O1203 715690.

Osmunda: Sizergh Castle (as Asplenium, above).

Polypodium: RHS Garden Harlow Carr (as Dryopteris, above)

Polypodium: Martin Rickard, Pear Tree Cottage, Kyre, Tenbury Wells, Worcestershire WR15 8 RN. Tel: 01885 410729.

Polystichum: Joan Loraine, Greencombe Gardens Trust, Porlock, Somerset TA24 8NU. Tel: 01643 862363.

Polystichum: Lakeland Horticultural Society, Holehird, Ullswater Road, Windermere, Cumbria LA23 1NP.

Selaginella. Stephan Czeladzinski, Barbican Conservatory, Barbican Centre, Silk Street, London EC2Y 8DS. Tel: 020 7638 6114.

France

General ferns (epiphytic) Conservatoire et Jardin Botanique de Nancy, 100 Rue du Jardin Botanique, 54600 Villers de Nancy.

General ferns: Mairie de Paris, Direction des Parcs, Jardins et Espaces Verts, 1 Avenue Gordon Bennett, 75016 Paris.

North America

There are no national collections as such, but fern collections have been set up all over the USA to establish hardiness in different areas. Contact the **Hardy Fern Foundation** for more information.

GLOSSARY

Acroscopic – side of pinna nearest frond tip.

Acutilobum – see *Polystichum setiferum* (p. 76).

Angustatum – narrow.

Antheridia – male sex organ on prothallus.

Antherozoid – male gamete.

Apospory – reproducing without spores.

Archegonia – female sex organ on prothallus.

Basiscopic – side of pinna furthest from frond tip.

Bifid – split into two.

Bipinnate – pinnae divided into distinct pinnules.

Bipinnate-pinnatifid – pinnules almost divided into pinnulets.

Calcareous – limey, usually relating to soil.

Capitatum – tip of frond crested, pinnae uncrested.

Caudex – fern stem, the rhizome.

Chromosome – components of cell nucleus carrying the inherited genetic material.

Congestum – overlapping pinnae and/or pinnules.

Crenate – roundly lobed margin.

Cristatum – tip of frond and pinnae crested, forked tips.

Crozier – uncurling frond.

Cruciate – cross-shaped.

Cultivar –cultivated variety.

Deltate – triangular.

Dentatum – shallow, regular teeth.

Depauperate – lacking parts.

Dimorphic – fronds or parts of fronds of two types.

Diploid – having two sets of chromosomes.

Divisilobum – see *Polystichum setiferum* (p. 76).

Epiphytic – growing on other plants, using them as a substrate (not parasitic).

Falcate – sickle-shaped, usually meaning the pinnae are curved towards tip of frond.

Flabellate – fan-shaped.

Foliose – leafy.

Genus (genera) – term for a group of closely related species.

Grandiceps – tip of frond crest broader than the frond, pinnae also crested.

Haploid – having one set of chromosomes.

Hybrid – result of a cross between two different taxa.

Incisum – margins deeply and irregularly indented.

Indusium – flap of tissue covering the sorus.

Lacerate – irregularly cut margin.

Lanceolate – lance-shaped, broadest between the middle and base.

Marginatum – fleshy ridges, parallel with the margin, usually along underside of frond.

Muricatum – pimpled frond surface.

Pedate – hand-shaped frond.

Pedate – hand-shaped frond.

Percristatum – cresting on frond, pinnae and pinnule tips.

Pinna (pinnae) – primary divisions of fronds.

Pinnate – frond divided into distinctly separate pinnae.

Pinnate-pinnatifid – pinnae almost divided into pinnules.

Pinnatifid – frond almost divided into pinnae.

Pinnules – divisions of pinnae.

Pinnulets – divisions of pinnules.

Plumoso-divisilobum – see *Polystichum setiferum* (p.76).

Plumoso multilobum – see *Polystichum setiferum* (p.76).

Plumosum – pinnules large, feathery, usually sterile.

Polydactylous – many-fingered.

Proliferous – bud-bearing.

Prothallus (prothalli) – alternative generation.

Quadripinnate – frond subdivided to fourth level.

Rachis – section of frond midrib that bears the leafy part of the frond.

Ramosum – branching, usually in bottom half of frond.

Rhizome – the fern's stem.

Serrate – margin regularly cut into fine teeth.

Setigerum – pinnules with bristles at tips.

Sorus (sori) – the spore-producing structure, contains sporangia.

Sporangium (sporangia) – structures containing spores.

Spore – dust-like particle that germinates to produce a prothallus.

Sporeling – young fern plant.

Stipe – midrib of frond, below the leafy part.

Stolon – short-lived creeping stem.

Taxon (taxa) – a unit of classification.

Tripinnate – pinnules divided into pinnulets.

Xerophyte – growing in dry habitats.

Selected bibliography

Brownsey, Patrick J. and Smith-Dodsworth, John C.,
New Zealand Ferns and Allied Plants, David Bateman, 1989.

Druery, Charles T., *British Ferns and their Varieties*,
Routledge, 1910.

Duncan, Betty D. and Isaac, Golda, *Ferns and Allied Plants
of Victoria, Tasmania and South Australia*, Melbourne, 1986.

Dyce, James W., *Fern Names and their Meanings*,
British Pteridological Society, 1988.

Dyce, James W., *The Cultivation and Propagation of British Ferns*,
British Pteridological Society, 1993.

Dyce, James W., *Variation in the genus* Polystichum *in the
British Isles*, 2003, in press.

Francis, George W., *An Analysis of the British Ferns and their Allies*,
London, 1837.

Goudey, Chris, *Maidenhair ferns in Cultivation*, Lothian, 1985.

Jones, David L., *Encyclopaedia of Ferns*, Lothian, Melbourne
and Timber Press, Oregon, 1987.

Kaye, Reginald, *Hardy Ferns*, Faber & Faber, 1968.

Lowe, Edward J., *Our Native Ferns*, Groombridge,
London, 1862–67.

Lowe, Edward J., *British Ferns and Where Found*,
Swan Sonnenschein, London, 1890.

Mickel, John T., *Ferns for American Gardens,* Macmillan, 1994.

Moore, Thomas E., *The Ferns of Great Britain and Ireland*,
London, 1855.

Newman, Edward, *A History of British Ferns*, London, 1840.

Newman, Edward, *A History of British Ferns,* London, 1844.

Newman, Edward, *A History of British Ferns,* Van Voorst, 1854.

Rickard, Martin H., *The Plantfinder's Guide to Garden Ferns*,
David & Charles, 2000.

Rush, Richard, *A Guide to Hardy Ferns*,
British Pteridological Society, 1984.

*The Victorian fernery at
Brodsworth Hall
Doncaster, Yorkshire, six
months after the entire
collection had been
transplanted from
Lancashire.*

INDEX

Page numbers in **bold** refer
to illustrations

Index compiled by Indexing Specialists (UK) Ltd.

Author Acknowledgements:

I would like to thank the following people for allowing me to take photographs in their private gardens:
Ann Bertie-Roberts, Worcesteshire; Clive and Doreen Brotherton, Staffordshire; Joyce Hayward, Staffordshire; Olive Mason, Worcestershire; John and Carol Mickel, New York State, USA; Roger and Sue Norman, Herefordshire; George and Grizel Williams; Shropshire.